CORE BELIEFS *of the* CHRISTIAN FAITH

by

Dr. J. Dalton Havard
Pastor Emeritus
Sugar Creek Baptist Church
Sugar Land, Texas

ISBN: 1-4196-7016-6
ISBN-13: 9781419670169

Printed in the United States of America
Visit www.booksurge.com to order additional copies.

ACKNOWLEDGEMENTS

I offer my sincere appreciation and enduring gratitude to my dear friends Dr. John R. Bisagno, Chuck Moritz, Tom Stewart, Dr. Clifford "Doc" Price, John Rushing, and Don Johnston for their wise counsel and indispensable assistance in making this book a reality.

Cover Design by | **Hector Sotelo**
Edited by | **Kaylan Christopher**

DEDICATION

It is with deep and abiding gratitude that I dedicate this volume to the Board of Directors of the J. Dalton Havard Evangelistic Association and the scores of others who made it possible for me to teach and preach the truths set forth therein to people on six continents.

They have been partners with me and our Lord Jesus Christ in carrying out His commission to be "...witnesses unto Me in Jerusalem, and in all Judea and Samaria, and to the ends of the earth."

TABLE OF CONTENTS

FOREWORD i

INTRODUCTION...v

THE BIBLE: The Authority for the Christian Faith 1

THEOLOGY: The Doctrine of God....................................13

CHRISTOLOGY: Who is Jesus of Nazareth? 25

PNEUMATOLOGY: The Doctrine of the Holy Spirit........ 37

ANTHROPOLOGY: The Doctrine of Man......................... 49

SOTERIOLOGY: The Doctrine of Salvation 55

ECCLESIOLOGY: The Doctrine of the Church 63

ESCHATOLOGY: The Doctrine of Last Things................. 85

MY TESTIMONY.. 101

FOREWORD

For years now, it has been the choice of many churches to forego serious attention to the basic doctrines of the Bible. Messages on positive thinking and felt needs have taken precedence over the deeper truths of Scripture. The end result has been the emergence of a generation that is essentially biblically illiterate. And while feel-good sermons felt good at the time, they have not provided the foundation for truth needed to live in the real world. Bible study classes and pulpits have become silent about the subject of doctrine. As a result, it has contributed to a generation that has replaced the personhood of God, according to biblical revelation, with their own imagination of who they want God to be.

It's no wonder such confusion abounds among believers about the nature of the Trinity, the awe of our salvation, our security and worth in Christ, our power for living through God's Holy Spirit, and so many other truths. The Bible has been displaced by pop psychology and current philosophies. However, our generation's plight isn't unique. In Hosea's time, God warned that His people were destroyed by a lack of knowledge about Him and His Word (Hosea 4:6). Is not the same thing happening today? Yet, the Lord says, "But on this one will I look: On him who is poor and of a contrite spirit, and who trembles at My Word" (Isaiah 66:2b).

Thank God for faithful shepherds who teach and live out the truths and principles found in His Word amidst such mayhem and confusion in our world today. Such a faithful shepherd is Dr. Dalton Havard, who has devotedly expounded the whole counsel of God during his entire 60-year ministry. For 10 of those 60 years, he pastored Sugar Creek Baptist Church in Sugar Land, Texas and today serves as our Pastor Emeritus. I lovingly call him our "resident theologian."

Among his many ministries, Pastor Havard prepares every deacon and ministerial candidate in our church for a rigorous ordination examination. He spends weeks teaching them the foundational truths of Scripture and helps them articulate those truths into their own words. And he has also taught all of our existing deacons and staff the same doctrinal lessons. We have now set him loose to teach doctrinal Bible study classes to our congregation. He, along with other pastors and teachers, is raising the level of knowledge and understanding about the precious doctrines of our faith among the members of Sugar Creek Baptist Church.

Pastor Havard has skillfully placed the deep truths of God's Word into a vernacular resource that all can understand and enjoy. Drawn from his many years of studying and communicating the Bible, he lays these doctrinal treasures out in the simplest terms. This book can be studied progressively from front to back, or any one particular doctrine can be easily selected to receive quick and accurate instruction. It will inspire, strengthen, and challenge you on your journey with God and others.

As I read it, I wished Christians everywhere could be blessed by it. Pastor Havard's work will enlarge your understanding of the Bible with basic, solid doctrines, and can be referred to throughout life as questions about the Christian faith surface. It is my hope that the Lord will illuminate your path with wisdom and understanding as you consume this work from the heart of a godly man I have the privilege of calling my friend. May the Lord's richest blessing be upon your life as you walk with Him.

Mark Hartman
Senior Pastor, Sugar Creek Baptist Church

INTRODUCTION

Many people yearn for answers to great spiritual questions that fill their minds and hearts. Often the answers provided by today's evangelical leaders do more to confuse than to clarify. In this book, I have set forth a summary of the fundamental doctrines of the Christian faith in language any layperson can understand.

The moral decay in our society has resulted in social and spiritual consequences never before experienced. Its tentacles have infiltrated all levels of our social system and it seems to possess the power to devour our treasured concepts and spiritual values.

Changes of this magnitude within a developed social structure usually take several generations. In our society, vast changes took place in only one generation. Dr. Clifford D. Price, in his treatise titled, "The Erosion of the American Christian Ethics," states:

> *Change in any society is necessary. A continued status quo will result in stagnation and eventually decay. But change must be slow in order for society to adjust to or reject its purpose. Unfortunately, it does not have to have the sanction of the majority—only the unrestrained determination of "the few." When social values come under attack and there are no strong, effective attempts to defend those values, a moral revolution surfaces. Born from frustration, deception, and general distrust of authority, this revolution will continue until the strongest are seated in power.*

Moral changes that struck our culture were too fast for positive "grass roots" reaction to block the advance. Established morals were adversely affected, and basic Christian principles, the primary target of this secular humanistic effort, were under ferocious attack. As a result of these constant attacks on Christianity, a popular myth was born: People, including Christians, are no longer interested in the doctrines of Christian faith.

This may be true for some, but there are still multitudes who want to know more about basic truths of the Christian faith. Bible-believing Christians must arm themselves with the knowledge of God's revealed truth.

Pontius Pilate Asked: "What is truth?"
Two millennia ago Pontius Pilate cynically asked what truth is and waited not for an answer. His attitude has been adopted by millions, including the pseudo-intellectual elite.

Winston Churchill, while discussing the frivolous attitude of many, once said, "Now and then a man stumbles on truth, then gets up and goes on his way." It is this frivolous attitude that has led us into spiritual and social decay. The changes we have seen in a few decades target the very core of Christian precepts.

Sadly, a glaring weakness among evangelicals is the failure to strive for a sound converted membership with intelligent convictions. Much of what goes on in too many churches has resulted in a faith that is grounded only an inch deep. We are challenged by numerous influential sources to defend our faith and far too many Christians are not equipped to do it.

As one critic has said, the faith of too many believers has been reduced to "a throb in their breast, a lump in their throat, and a twinge in their conscience, but a vacuum in their heads."

It is my conviction that the Christian faith is based upon eternal, unchanging truths which have survived the assaults of atheists, agnostics, and countless other enemies. Christians must do a better job of proclaiming and defending these truths in a society where humanism has become the "state religion." This philosophy has launched this generation into a turbulent sea without a compass, without a rudder, and without an anchor.

THE BIBLE: The Authority
for the Christian Faith

The Christian faith is not based on experiences. Though, Christian experience is important. Nor is the Christian faith based on human knowledge—although the Apostle Paul commanded us to "study to show ourselves approved unto God," and to "present [ourselves] to God… which is [our] reasonable service."

The Christian faith is based upon the Bible—that which Christians believe to be the inspired Word of God.

Creeds, or the proclamations of men that are adopted by church bodies in many cases, are valuable statements of essential truth. A good example is found in Dr. B.H. Carroll's book, "Inspiration of the Bible," which states:

> *We believe the Holy Bible was written by men divinely inspired, and is a perfect treasure of heavenly instruction: that it has God for its author, salvation for its end, and truth without any mixture of error for its matter; that it reveals the principles by which God will judge us; and therefore is, and shall remain to the end of the world, the*

*true center of Christian union, and the supreme standard
by which all human conduct, creeds, and opinions shall
be tried.*

However, creeds are not our ultimate authority. Papal pronouncements, or pronouncements of church councils, are not the source of the ultimate authority of the Christian faith. Our faith is based upon the Bible—God's verbally-inspired, inerrant word to us.

It is not my purpose to prove the authenticity of the Bible. There are many rich scholarly resources available to demonstrate its credibility and authenticity. One fine source is a booklet titled, "The Facts of Why You Can Believe the Bible," by John Ankerberg and John Weldon. And another is "Faith on Trial" by Pamela Bennings Ewen, in which she points out that archaeological, historical, scientific, documentary, and medical evidence is such that it would be allowed in any court in America.

Professor F.F. Bruce noted, "If the New Testament were a collection of secular writings, their authority would generally be regarded as beyond doubt."

The greatest scholar I ever studied under was Dr. Bernard Ramm. He was my professor (and also my close friend) of systematic theology in graduate school at Baylor University. Dr. Ramm said, regarding the attempt across the centuries to destroy the authenticity of the Bible:

*A thousand times over, the death knell of the Bible has been
sounded, the funeral procession formed, the inscription cut
on the tombstone, and the committal read. But somehow
the corpse never stays put.*

If one asks, "Is there absolute evidence that verifies our conviction that the Bible is the Word of God?" The answer is "no"—the evidence is quite good, but it is not absolute. Many scholars believe God planned it that way. His desire is for His people to exercise FAITH in Him for "…without faith it is impossible to please Him" (Hebrews 11:6).

Faith in the validity and authority of Scripture is essential to the Christian. Otherwise, our faith would be no different than that of the pagan religions of the world. It would be nothing more than blind obedience.

However, it is not a "blind leap of faith." Internal evidence in the Bible is sufficient to convince any honest and objective seeker of truth that the Bible has been given to us by divine revelation from the only true God of the universe.

FULFILLED PROPHECY
Scores of prophecies fulfilled hundreds of years ago, to the smallest detail, after they were given, should say something about the validity of Scripture.

In one day—the day Jesus was crucified—at least 29 specific prophecies written at least 500 years earlier were literally fulfilled. Consider the following examples:

- He will be betrayed by a friend (Ps. 41:9; Matt. 26:49).
- The price of His betrayal will be 30 pieces of silver (Zach. 11:12; Matt. 26:15).
- The betrayal money will be cast to the floor of the temple (Zach. 11:13; Matt. 27:5)
- He will be forsaken by His disciples (Zach. 13:7; Mark 14:50).
- He will be silent before His accusers (Is. 53:7; Matt. 27:12).

- He will be wounded and bruised (Is. 53:5; Matt. 27:26).
- He will be struck and spit on (Is. 53:6; Matt. 26:67).
- He will be taunted with specific words (Ps. 22:6-8; Matt. 27:39-43).
- He will be executed among sinners (Is. 53:12; Matt. 27:38).
- His hands and feet will be pierced (Ps. 22:16; Luke 23:33).
- He will thirst (Ps. 69:21; John 19:28).
- His bones will be left unbroken (Ps. 34:20; John 19:33).
- His heart will rupture (Ps. 22:14; John 19:34).
- His side will be pierced (Zach. 12:10; John 19:34).
- He will be buried in a rich man's tomb (Is. 53:9; Matt. 27:57-60).

Professor Peter W. Stoner states that the probability of just eight prophecies being fulfilled in one person's life is 1 in 100,000,000,000,000,000. The Bible is the authority used in this dissertation to present a simple summary of the basic truths of the Christian faith.

Scripture is not the musings or philosophizingof men.

FACTS ABOUT THE BIBLE

The Bible is really a library containing a collection of 66 books—39 in the Old Testament and 27 in the New Testament. The Old Testament was written primarily in the Hebrew language, while the New Testament was written in the Greek language. And each has been translated into every major language of the world.

It was written over a period of 1,500 years by 40 different writers during many different cultures of those times, yet without contradiction. The Bible is the inerrant revelation of

God Himself to mankind, and was written by men under the inspiration of the Holy Spirit.

The Apostle Peter wrote, "...prophecy never came by the will of man, but holy men of God spoke as they were moved by the Holy Spirit" (2 Peter 1:21). And the Apostle Paul wrote, "All Scripture is given by inspiration of God" (2 Timothy 3:16).

Scripture is not the musings or philosophizing of men. It is God communicating to man His will, His way, His desire, and His design for mankind for His glory and mankind's good. It is miraculously given. An example: In some of His final words to His disciples, Jesus told them, "The Holy Spirit...will teach you all things and bring to your remembrance all things I said to you" (John 14:26).

Years later, some apostles wrote down what Jesus had said to them. Can you remember verbatim the sermon your pastor preached last week? Can you remember verbatim a conversation you had with your spouse two months ago?

The fact that these men were able to recall, word-for-word, the teachings of Jesus Christ many months after His resurrection, is a miraculous work of the Holy Spirit. If Christianity is unique among the religions of the world, then it requires Divine affirmation. It must have a greater authority than just the opinions of men—regardless of their sincerity or intellect.

The Bible, therefore, is our textbook, our revelation of truth. It is our only authentic source of knowledge about God and our Savior Jesus Christ. Nature gives us evidences of a Supernatural Being, but reveals nothing about His character and attributes. Only the Bible reveals the personal characteristics of God. For instance, the Bible makes this astonishing statement: "God is love." Where else would mankind ever come up with that idea?

Christians profess that Jesus of Nazareth is the Eternal Christ, the Incarnate Son of God. Jesus Himself claimed the Bible to be the Word of God (see Luke 24:27, 44-45). So how can we believe Him to be all He claimed to be and not accept His affirmation of the Bible as the Word of God? Some skeptics will say, "There have been many who have claimed to be the Christ, or who claim to be divine."

Yes, but did they validate it by rising from the dead after being buried for three days?

THREE THEORIES OF INSPIRATION
Christian scholars have proposed many theories of inspiration, with the following three being the most common:

Partial Inspiration
This theory teaches that only parts of the Bible are inspired. For example, the Apostle Paul says in Second Timothy 3:16: "All Scripture is given by inspiration of God…"

Partial theory translates this verse, "All Scripture that is inspired of God…" If this theory is correct, then we must have someone who is inspired by the Holy Spirit to let us know which part of the Bible *is* inspired.

Mechanical Inspiration
This theory teaches that men who wrote Scripture were only secretaries taking dictation. I do not accept this because it ignores the obvious fact that different writers used different styles and vocabularies to present the same truths.

Dynamic, Plenary, and Verbal

This theory satisfies my understanding of how God gave us the Bible without error because:

- It is dynamic, meaning that God chose certain men and used their personalities, minds, and experiences to write exactly what He wanted written.

- It is plenary, meaning that "all Scripture is given by inspiration," or God-breathed. The entire Bible is not equally valuable, but all of it is equally inspired.

- It is verbal, meaning that every word of the original text was inspired by the Holy Spirit. You cannot express ideas, or declare truth and explain it without words. Therefore, I believe in the verbal inspiration of the Bible.

LITERAL OR SYMBOLIC?

I firmly believe that the Bible should be interpreted literally except where it is obviously symbolic.

There are many figures of speech used in the Bible, but when you read them in a larger context and in light of Scripture as a whole, it is not difficult to see the difference between literal and symbolic. For example, Jesus said that God is a Spirit. Yet Psalms 91:4 says, "He shall cover you with His feathers and under His wings you shall take refuge."

This sounds like God is a big bird! Yet the context clearly reveals that the psalmist was speaking metaphorically of God as our refuge and our protector. Several times the Bible speaks of the "hand" of God. This sounds like God is a man.

Yet these references show that the writers are describing the power, might, and authority of God.

Taking a passage out of its context is a dangerous way to study the Bible. Scripture must be studied in large segments if we are to properly understand it. One can take a verse out of its context and prove anything he desires to, such as the example shown above.

The Bible declares more than 2500 times that God spoke directly to men.

The men who wrote the Bible wrote exactly what God wanted as they were "moved along" by the Holy Spirit. Today, we are paying the price of decades of scoffing at the Bible and its relevancy in our society. We have been inundated with the secular humanistic philosophy of life, or life with no regard for God and His Word, and we are reaping the bitter fruit.

Dr. B. H. Carroll, one of America's spiritual and intellectual giants, wrote: *"Whenever you sow a nation down with the heathen theory as applied to the Bible, you may look for a crop of anarchy..."*

We see, in our generation, the results of decades of slander against the Bible and against those who practice its teachings.

ILLUMINATION OF THE HOLY SPIRIT
The Bible says, in 1 Corinthians 2:14, that Scripture cannot be understood without the "illumination" of the Holy Spirit:

"The natural (unregenerate man) does not receive the things of the Spirit of God, for they are foolishness to him; nor can he know them, because they are spiritually discerned."

The word "foolishness" in this verse is translated from the Greek word "moro" from which we get our word moronic. To the skeptical unbeliever, the Bible is foolishness, but to the believer, it contains the words of life.

The Holy Spirit illumines—makes clear and understandable —the great truths of God's revelation to mankind. In His last instructions to His disciples, Jesus said that the Holy Spirit would be their teacher and helper (John 14:25-26).

> ***The Bible is given to us to reveal God and His redemption in and through Jesus Christ.***

THE PURPOSE OF THE BIBLE

The Bible is given to us to reveal God and His redemption in and through Jesus Christ. All that we know about the true, eternal God of the universe, we learn first from the Bible.

The idea of God is not the result of the searching and reasoning of man. It is God revealing Himself to man. The Bible reveals not only that God is real, but also what He is like. The Bible reveals truths we could never know otherwise.

For example, the Bible uses the term "mystery" many times. The word mystery (Greek = "musterion") in the Bible does not refer to a riddle. It refers to a truth that could never be discovered except by the revelation from God.

An excellent example of this is found in Colossians 1:27: "… God willed to make known what are the riches of the glory of this mystery among the Gentiles: which is Christ in you, the hope of glory."

Who would ever have thought that God or Jesus Christ could dwell in a person? God may be perceived to be above us, in front of us, or beside us, but not in us.

The Bible reveals God's plan of redemption, not only for sinful man, but for the earth (Romans 8:16-22). Only in the Bible do we find God's plan to redeem sinful man.

Someone may say, "The Bible is not logical." I agree. It is not logical that the eternal God of the universe would come down to this earth, be incarnate in a man, and die on a cross to pay the penalty for the sins of mankind. But praise His holy name that He did!

The Bible reveals what we are as human beings. We are God's creation. We are rebellious, sinful people in need of a Savior. This will be discussed more thoroughly in chapter five.

The Bible reveals God's expectations of us. He created us for His own glory. He created us with the ability and responsibility to choose what we will do with His revealed will.

We are not spiritual and intellectual robots. He reveals Himself and His truth. We glorify Him when we freely choose to believe and follow Him in and through Jesus Christ. He has redeemed the believer to be conformed to the image of Jesus Christ. (Philippians 3:21).

The Bible tells us what we are to believe and how we are to behave. It reveals how we are to be saved, how we are to live, and where we will spend eternity.

How blessed mankind is that God did not leave us in the dark to find our own way. He has revealed Himself and given us a blueprint for a full and meaningful life here and throughout eternity. Read it to be *wise*. Believe it to be *saved*. Practice it to have *joy* and *peace*.

2

THEOLOGY: The Doctrine of God

The Bible does not attempt to prove the existence of God. It opens with a simple statement, "In the beginning God…" It reveals God as the only infinite and eternal being.

God is not discovered by natural reasoning. Scripture says, "He that comes to God must believe that He is…" (Hebrews 11:6). This does not mean that we are not to use our minds.

In many places throughout the Bible, we are exhorted to study, reason, and analyze the scriptures. It does mean that the true, infinite, and personal God of the universe could not and would not have been discovered except as God revealed Himself to mankind.

This He has done as the following Scripture in Hebrews 1:1-2 indicates:

> *"God, who at various times and in various ways spoke in time past to the fathers by the prophets, as in these last days spoken to us by His Son…"*

The Psalmist said, "The fool has said in his heart there is no God" (Psalm 14:1), but genuine Christians believe there is only one "living and true God" (1 Thessalonians 1:9).

Isaiah 46:9 says, "I am God, and there is none else; I am God, and there is none like me." Christians believe the Bible to be the inspired Word of God, and the Bible clearly teaches the eternal existence of the universal, eternal, personal God.

EVIDENCES OF GOD

In Nature
The magnitude, majesty, and complexity of the universe (which I believe to be infinite) give evidence of an all-wise and all-powerful God.

"The heavens declare the glory of God; and the skies proclaim the work of His hands" (Psalm 19:1).

Scientists tell us that the sun is 93 million miles from the earth and the nearest star is a trillion miles from the earth. There are at least 250 million times 250 million stars in our galaxy. Surely, this requires an intelligent, powerful creator whom we call God.

In Logic
Everything that began owes its existence to a cause. A building requires a builder, and a watch demands a watchmaker.

I once heard a story about a man who showed a little boy his watch and said, "Do you know where I got this watch? I was walking down a road and all of a sudden various pieces of this watch started falling from the sky and all these pieces came together and made this watch."

The little boy responded, "Are you crazy or something?"

Also, in the movie "The Sound of Music" Maria sings, "Nothing comes from nothing. Nothing ever did."

This universe could no more come into existence without an intelligent creator than the alphabet could produce a book without an author.

In Anthropology

Anthropology (the Doctrine of Man) gives evidence of God. Man is different from everything else that lives:

- He is moral and spiritual by nature.
- He is a living soul with the capacity to make moral and spiritual decisions.
- He has the ability to determine the difference between right and wrong.
- He has the ability to make spiritual decisions and receive and respond to the revelations of God.

Surely, this is evidence of God. No other creature on earth has such ability.

To try and define God is like attempting to put Niagara Falls into a thimble. It is impossible.

THE ATTRIBUTES OF GOD

To try and define God is like attempting to put Niagara Falls into a thimble. It is impossible. Our God is infinite. He is too awesome and majestic for us to fully describe, and I am glad for that!

To use His own words: "For as the heavens are higher than the earth, so are My ways higher than your ways, and My thoughts higher than your thoughts" (Isaiah 55:9).

His Names

One way to attempt to describe Him is to use some of the various names the Bible uses for God:

- **Elohim – "The Powerful God"**
  "In the beginning God created the heavens and the earth" (Genesis 1:1). "In the beginning" shows us that God is eternal and "created" shows His power.
- **El Elyon – "God Most High"**
  He is the highly exalted One (see Genesis 14: 19-20).
- **El Shaddai – "The Almighty One"**
  Nothing is beyond His power and ability. God has infinite resources to supply all our needs (see Genesis 17:1).
- **Yahweh, or Jehovah – "Israel's Covenant God"**
  This is the Name God gave Himself: "I Am WHO I Am" (Exodus 3:14). I Am is what He has always been—the eternal God of the universe.

"I am the LORD (Yahweh); that is my name! I will not give my glory to another or my praise to idols" (Isaiah 42:8). Yahweh is His redemptive name, and he gave this name to Himself in making His covenant with Moses to redeem Israel from Egyptian slavery. Jesus took this same name (see John 8:58) in claiming to be the eternal Messiah, our Savior and Redeemer.

He is a Person

The Bible reveals God as a person, not just an impersonal power. He is called "the living and true God" (1 Thessalonians

1:9). He is revealed as one having self-consciousness and self-determination.

He loves (John 3:16). He hates (Proverbs 6:16). He cares (1 Peter 5:7). He grieves (Genesis 6:6). Only a personality can love, hate, care, and grieve. Therefore, God is a person.

He is One God
There is one God who revealed Himself as God the Father, God the Son, and God the Holy Spirit (Deuteronomy 6:4; Mark 12:29).

One of the early church's creeds states, "Within the nature of God there are three persons, Father, Son, and Holy Spirit; and these three persons share the same attributes. In fact these three persons are one God."

Christians have been accused of worshiping three Gods; that is not true. We believe there is ONE God who has revealed Himself as the Trinity—three distinct personalities: Father, Son, Holy Spirit.

Admittedly, this is a difficult truth to explain. Let us look at it this way: not as $1 + 1 + 1 = 3$, but as $1 \times 1 \times 1 = 1$. A good example is the chemical formula H_2O. Ask a first-year chemistry student to give the definition of H_2O, and he will answer that it is "water." But what about it's form?

What if the temperature is below freezing? It is not a fluid, but a solid. What if the temperature is above the boiling point? It is not a fluid, but steam. It is the same thing (H_2O), but it is manifested in three different forms. Christians worship one God who has revealed Himself in three forms as the Father, Son, and Holy Spirit.

We are born and we die.
There are no such limitations on God.

He is Eternal

He is from everlasting to everlasting. He transcends our understanding of time. He had no beginning and will have no end. We place biological limitations on man. We are born and we die. There are no such limitations on God.

The scripture says, "In the beginning God..." When everything else had its beginning, God was already there. And scripture also says, "Now to the King eternal, immortal, invisible, to God who alone is wise, be honor and glory forever and ever (1 Timothy 1:17).

He is Changeless

This is what theologians call the immutability of God. He never changes. "I am the Lord, I do not change....." (Malachi 3:6). The poet, Thomas Chisholm, expressed it so beautifully:

> *"Great is Thy faithfulness, O God my Father. There is no shadow of turning with Thee. Thou changest not, Thy compassions they fail not. As Thou hast been, Thou forever will be."*

Isn't it wonderful that our God does not act in response to public opinion polls? His standard of righteousness does not fluctuate and is not influenced by popular mores. He is our lighthouse to lead us through the storms of life.

God is Holy

The Psalmist said, "Exalt the Lord (Yahweh) our God and worship at His holy hill; for the Lord (Yahweh) our God is holy" (Psalm 99:9).

Holiness refers to God's purity. He is totally, absolutely pure from all imperfections. He is called "light" and in Him there is no darkness at all. None of God's attributes are sounded out so loftily, and with such solemnity as is His holiness. The angels (see Isaiah 6:3) sounded out His praises by singing, "Holy, Holy, Holy is the Lord of hosts; the whole earth is full of His glory!"

I once heard a television reporter arrogantly assert, "I could interview God and not be intimated."

I thought, "You poor soul. That's because you don't have the slightest idea of who you are interviewing!"

If she had ever been given the opportunity, she would have done as Isaiah did. She would have fallen on her face before our Holy God and said, "Woe is me, for I am undone…for my eyes have seen the King, the Lord (Yahweh) of hosts" (Isaiah 6:5).

He is Spirit
The Apostle John said, "No one has seen God at any time…" (John 1:18; see also 1 John 4:12). Yet we see in Genesis 32:30 these words, "So Jacob called the name of the place Peniel: "For I have seen God face to face…"

Other passages, such as Exodus 24:10 and 33:33, confirm this.

The Scofield Reference Bible notes correctly clarify this seeming contradiction:

> *"The divine essence, God, in His own triune Person, no human being in the flesh has seen. But God, veiled in angelic form, and especially as incarnate in Jesus Christ, has been seen by man."*

The Eternal Spirit God has accommodated us by revealing Himself in physical form for our own benefit; but the spiritual essence of the totality of God no person in human flesh has seen.

He is Perfect in All His Ways
He is Omnipotent, meaning all-powerful. Jesus said of God, "With men this is impossible, but with God all things are possible" (Matthew 19:26). When the angel announced to the Mary that she was to give birth to a son, she argued with him saying, "How can this be, since I do not know (sexually) a man?" (Luke 1:34). The angel responded, "For with God nothing is impossible" (Luke 1:37).

He is Omniscient, meaning all-wise and all-knowledgeable. All of Psalm 139 is a magnificent discourse on this subject. Hebrews 4:13 declares, "And there is no creature hidden from His sight; but all things are naked and open to the eyes of Him to whom we must give account."

He is Omnipresent, meaning He is everywhere. "Where can I go from Your Spirit? Or where can I flee from Your presence?" (Psalm 139:7).

I heard the story of two American soldiers who were prisoners of war in a Nazi prison camp. They both were in isolation in adjoining cells, but they learned to communicate with each other by tapping their messages in Morse code on the wall that separated them.

One was a Christian, while the other was not. One day the non-Christian tapped out the message, "It's hell to be alone with one's self."

The Christian responded, "It is heaven to be alone with one's Lord."

God is not IN everything or else one could worship objects; but God IS everywhere present. What a wonderful reality!

I was in the airport in Osaka, Japan in 1963, on my way from Tokyo to Fukuoka, on the Southern Island of Kyushu, for a preaching mission. The airport in Fukuoka was weathered in, and my flight was canceled.

Here I was thousands of miles away from home where absolutely no one knew me. I could not communicate with those around me. I was alone in a city of six million people. But I remembered the promise of our Lord, "...I am with you always, even to the end of the age" (Matthew 28:20).

He has proven His love once for all in giving us His Son, Jesus Christ, to die on the cross that He might save us from our sins.

God is Love

Perhaps the most encouraging revelation of God to sinful mankind is found in 1 John 4:8: "...God is love." However, the most memorized verse in the entire Bible is John 3:16.

The most interesting translation of that verse I ever heard came from the lips of a drunken man, 15,000 feet above sea level in the Andes Mountains is Cuzco, Peru—the capitol city of the ancient Inca Indian empire.

There is not a single evangelical church in this city; but our group heard of a Christian bookstore there. Late one evening we asked our guide, who by this time was pretty well inebriated, to take us there.

When we got there, we found the store closed. On the doorpost was a bronze plaque with a message in Spanish. Here was our guide's translation into English:

> *"God loved the world very much. So much that He gave the only Son He had that if any one would believe in Him he would stop dying and begin to live forever"* (John 3:16).

Many think of God as a "kill joy" waiting around to zap them. But the only true God, the Creator of the universe, including mankind, is a God of love. He has proven His love once for all in giving us His Son, Jesus Christ, to die on the cross that He might save us from our sins. Love is not God; but GOD IS LOVE.

One of the most thrilling verses in the Bible is this: "But God demonstrates His own love toward us, in that while we were still sinners, Christ died for us" (Romans 5:8). Frederick M. Lehman wrote a hymn in 1917 titled "The Love of God." One verse stated:

> *"Could we with ink the ocean fill, and were the skies of parchment made, were every stalk on earth a quill, and every man a scribe by trade, to write the love of God above would drain the ocean dry. Nor could the scroll contain the whole, though stretched from sky to sky."*

God is Faithful

Our Loving God is always faithful. He is faithful to keep His promises, and He keeps His promise to forgive. And since our God is Holy and expects holiness from us, there is nothing mankind needs more than forgiveness.

The Bible says, and experience confirms, that "…all have sinned and fall short of the glory of God" (Romans 3:23), and that "the wages of sin is death" (Romans 6:23). But, thanks be to our Lord, that the second part of that verse says "the gift of God is eternal life in Christ Jesus our Lord" (Romans 6:23).

The Apostle John wrote, under inspiration of the Holy Spirit, "If we confess our sins, He is faithful and just to forgive us our sins and to cleanse us from all unrighteousness" (1 John 1:9). He keeps His promise to always strengthen, give guidance, encourage, and comfort us. The Bible, "...I will never leave you nor forsake you" (Hebrews 13:5).

I had a wonderful affirmation of this promise which I will never forget when I went on a month-long mission trip to Brazil. Flying across the Gulf of Mexico, totally exhausted both physically and emotionally, I looked out the window of the plane. There were clouds in the sky. Some rain was falling in the distance, and below our plane was a rainbow.

Looking from above, a rainbow is a perfect circle. Right in the center of that rainbow was the shadow of our plane. I said, "Thank you, Lord, for reminding me of your constant presence in every experience and condition of life."

What an awesome God we have! Oftentimes in my private prayer I ask Him to give me a growing understanding of His majesty and glory. How humbling and sobering it is to spend time meditating on what it will be like standing in the presence of the eternal, all wise, all powerful, Holy God of the universe!

Only in Christ will be permitted to stand there accepted. Listen to His word in Jude 24:25 and Jude 1:25:

"Now to Him Who is able to keep you from stumbling, and to present you faultless before the presence of His glory with exceed joy. ... To God our Savior, Who alone is wise, be glory and majesty, dominion and power, both now and forever. Amen."

Let us trust Him, love Him, obey Him, follow Him, and find LIFE in its fullness here and forever.

3

CHRISTOLOGY: Who is Jesus?

*Either this man was, and is, the Son of God: or else a
madman or something worse*

The two most important questions ever asked of mankind
are these: "What do you think about the Christ? Whose Son
is He?" (Matthew 22:42) and "What then shall I do with Jesus
who is called the Christ?" (Matthew 27:22).

These are the pivotal questions for the mind of any person
who would know the eternal God of the universe. Who is this
person who has been described as "The central character of
history?"

There is a fascination with Jesus Christ that we find in no
other person who ever lived. After 20 centuries, Jesus is still
the disturbing, surprising, fascinating Master of men. Even
skeptics cannot get Him out of their minds.

Nowhere is His influence summed up better than in "One
Solitary Life":

"All the armies that ever marched, and all the navies that ever sailed, and all the parliaments that ever sat, and all the kings that ever reigned, put together, have not affected the life of mankind on this earth as powerfully as has that One Solitary Life."

Napoleon, the exiled emperor on the lonely isle of St. Helena, was discussing Christ with General Bertrand who followed him into banishment. Napoleon said:

"I know men, and I tell you that Jesus Christ is not a man. Superficial minds see a resemblance between Christ and the founders of empires and the gods of other religions. That resemblance does not exist. There is between Christianity and whatever other religions the distance of infinity. ... Everything in Christ astonishes me. His spirit overawes me, and His will confounds me..."

Jean-Jacques Rousseau, Swiss philosopher and writer, said of Him, "If the life and death of Socrates were those of a sage, the life and death of Jesus are those of a God."

Ian Maclaren, Scottish author and theologian, said of those who try to rate Jesus Christ with sages, such as Buddha, Muhammad, or Zoroaster, "...It is as if one should compare the sun with an electric light bulb..."

THE INCARNATE ONE

Scripture proclaims that Jesus of Nazareth was the incarnation of the eternal God in human flesh. Any Christology short of this is heresy. This is what Jesus said about Himself to the woman at the well: "I who speak to you am He (the Christ)" (John 4:25-26).

In one of His confrontations with the hostile Pharisees—the self-righteous religious leaders of His day—Jesus proclaimed that He was the eternal Christ: "Before Abraham was born, I AM" (John 8:58). He took the very name that God gave Himself (see Exodus 3:14).

Four of His Apostles, all monotheistic Jews (those who believe there is only one God), said of Him:

- The Apostle Peter proclaimed, "Thou art the Christ, the Son of the living God." Jesus commended him and told him that the Father in heaven had revealed this to him (Matthew 16:15-17).
- The Apostle John said, "In the beginning was the Word, and the Word was with God, and the Word was God. ... The Word became flesh and made His dwelling among us..." (John 1:1,14).
- The doubting Apostle Thomas, upon seeing Jesus for the first time after His resurrection, cried out, "My Lord and my God!" (John 20:28).
- The Apostle Paul, a converted monotheistic Jew, said of Him: "For in Christ all the fullness of the Deity lives in bodily form (Colossians 2:9).

C.S. Lewis, professor at Cambridge in England, writes:

> *"I am trying here to prevent anyone saying the really foolish thing that people often say about Him: 'I'm ready to accept Jesus as a great moral teacher, but I don't accept His claim to be God.' That is the one thing we must not say. A man who was merely a man and said the sort of things Jesus said would not be a great moral teacher. He would either be a lunatic–on the level with the man who says he is a poached egg–or else he would be the Devil of Hell. You must make your choice. Either this man was, and is, the Son of*

*God: or else a madman or something worse. You can shut
Him up for a fool, you can spit at Him and kill Him as a
demon, or you can fall at His feet and call Him Lord and
God. But let us not come with any patronizing nonsense
about Him being a great human teacher. He has not left
that open to us. He did not intend to."*

Josh McDowell, like C.S. Lewis, was formerly agnostic and
came, after serious research, to embrace Jesus Christ as God
incarnate. He said:

*"If, when Jesus made His claims, He knew He was not God,
then He was lying and deliberately deceiving His followers.
But if He was a liar, then He was also a hypocrite because
He told others to be honest, whatever the cost, while He
Himself taught and lived a colossal lie. More than that,
He was a demon, because He told others to trust Him for
their eternal destiny. If He couldn't back up His claims
and knew it, then He was unspeakably evil. Last, He
would also be a fool because it was His claim to being God
that led to His crucifixion."*

There is going on, as I write this, a resurgence of Gnostic
writings, such as the publication of "The Gospel of Judas."
And much of the heretical book titled "The Da Vinci Code"
is based upon the writings of the Gnostics.

The word "Gnosticism" comes from the Greek word "gnosis"
which means "knowledge." Gnosticism was a philosophy that
began to develop near the end of the first century. Their
basic theses were that only spirit is good and all matter is evil.
They taught that religious experience was authenticated by
the secret rites of the Gnostics.

Devotees of this philosophy began infiltrating the early church and became a serious threat to the fellowship and teachings of the apostles. They taught that Jesus could not be divine because He lived in a physical body.

One group of the Gnostics, known as Docetists (Greek: "dokein" meaning "to seem") taught that Jesus was not really a man. He just "seemed" to be a man. While professing to be Christians, they denied the incarnation. Another group of Gnostics—followers of the teachings of Cerinthus, a first century Gnostic—taught that Jesus was the offspring of a sexual union between Mary and Joseph.

According to them, divinity came upon Jesus at His baptism and left Him just before His crucifixion. Therefore, Jesus was not fully divine. There were scores of writings of the Gnostics in the second and third centuries, such as "The Gospel of Judas," all of which were rejected by the early church because of their heretical teachings.

For instance, this heretical gospel says that Jesus was married to Mary Magdalene, and they had a child. And it also claims that Jesus asked Judas to arrange His arrest and death so that He could be delivered from the prison of His body.

Many modern day atheists, agnostics, and skeptics are using these writings to denigrate the authenticity of scripture and make Jesus just another religious leader with feet of clay.

The Apostle John, in his dealings with these philosophers, called them "antichrists" (1 John 2:18, 22; 4:3).

JESUS: BORN OF A VIRGIN
The great prophet Isaiah wrote, "Therefore the Lord Himself

will give you a sign: The virgin will be with child and will give birth to a son, and will call him Immanuel" (Isaiah 7:14).

Seven hundred years later, an angel of God appeared to a young Jewish virgin and said to her:

> *"Do not be afraid, Mary, you have found favor with God. You will be with child and give birth to a son, and you are to give him the name Jesus. He will be great and will be called the Son of the Most High. The Lord God will give him the throne of his father David, and he will reign over the house of Jacob forever; his kingdom will never end. ... The Holy Spirit will come upon you, and the power of the Most High will overshadow you. So the holy one to be born will be called the Son of God"* (Luke 1:30-33, 35).

I can hear the skeptic ask, "If a young pregnant girl came to you and said, 'I am going to have a baby but I am a virgin,' would you believe her?"

My answer is: "If her baby were going to live a perfect life, give sight to a man born blind, walk on water, calm the raging sea by only speaking a word, raise a man from a grave who had been dead four days, voluntarily submit to a cruel Roman cross, and three days later rise from the dead—if her baby were going to live to do all this—then I would believe."

Jesus of Nazareth was, and is eternal deity, one with the Father and the Holy Spirit.

THE ATONING SACRIFICE FOR SIN

Jesus was the atoning sacrifice for sin. The Bible clearly teaches that "the wages of sin is death" (Romans 6:23). It also teaches that "all have sinned and fall short of the glory of God" (Romans 3:23).

The Bible makes it very clear that only by the atoning sacrifice of Jesus Christ is there forgiveness of sin (Hebrews 9:11-14, 22; 10:10-17; 1 John 1:7; Ephesians 1:7).

The poet and author of the gospel hymn, "Jesus Paid It All," Elvina M. Hall sang out:

> *"Jesus paid it all.*
> *All to Him I owe;*
> *Sin had left a crimson stain.*
> *He washed it white as snow. "*

When Jesus died on the cross, He bore in His body the sin of the whole world and paid the penalty of it in full. "God made Him who knew no sin to be sin for us, so that in Him we might become righteousness of God" (2 Corinthians 5:21). See also 1 Peter 1:18-19; 2:24.

Can you imagine what it must have been like for Jesus? He was the only man who ever lived a perfectly pure and sinless life and was made to carry our sin, in all its filthiness, hate, and hostility. No wonder He cried out in the Garden of Gethsemane, "If it is possible, may this cup be taken from me" (Matthew 26:29).

The scripture that best describes the horror of Jesus hanging on the cross of Calvary was written by the prophet Isaiah more than seven hundred years before His crucifixion (Isaiah 53). He was crushed, bruised, and beaten so badly that He hardly resembled a man.

The heart of every person who ever lived should sing out with the poet:

"I saw one hanging on a tree in agony and blood.
He fixed His languid eyes on me, as by His cross I stood.
O, can it be that on that tree the Savior died for me?
My soul is thrilled, my heart if filled,
To think He died for me. "

In the words of a famous news commentator, Paul Harvey: "Now for the rest of the story."

HIS RESURRECTION FROM THE DEAD

The Christian doctrine of the resurrection of Jesus Christ from the dead is the pivotal doctrine of the Christian faith. His bodily resurrection:

- Vindicates His claim to deity.
- Validates His substitutionary suffering on the cross.
- Vitalizes His priestly ministry.
- Vanquishes death for His people.
- Verifies His promise to come again.

The evidences of His resurrection are as convincing as the evidences that a historical person named Jesus Christ ever lived. Let us examine some of those evidences.

Post Resurrection Appearances:

When Jesus rose from the dead, He did not just mysteriously disappear. The Bible records at least nine post-resurrection appearances of Jesus to:

- Mary Magdalene on Sunday morning (John 20:14-18).
- The women returning from the empty tomb that same morning (Matthew 28:6-10).
- Peter, probably Sunday afternoon (Luke 24:34).
- Two disciples on the road to Emmaus the same Sunday

afternoon (Luke 24:13-31).
- The Apostles, except Thomas, the same evening (Luke 24:36-43).
- The Apostles, including Thomas, eight days later (John 20:24-29).
- The Apostles in Galilee (John 21:1-23).
- The Apostles in Jerusalem and Bethany again (Mark 16:14-20; Acts 1:3-12).
- More than 500 people at one time (1 Corinthians 15:6).

Some suggest that those who saw Jesus after His resurrection were hallucinating. But what credible psychologist would defend the idea that 500 people would hallucinate about the same thing at the same time?

In addition to these mentioned above, Jesus made three appearances to three different people after His ascension back to the Father:

- Saul of Tarsus (later called Paul) on the road to Damascus (Acts 9:6; 1 Corinthians 15:5-8).
- Stephen, the first Christian martyr (Acts 7:55).
- The Apostle John on the Isle of Patmos (Revelation 1:10-19).

> *The empty tomb is the most convincing evidence*
> *of all that Jesus arose from the dead.*

I heard a story about a missionary to northern India who had just finished preaching in a market place when a Muslim came up to him and said, "You must admit that we have one thing you do not have."

The missionary asked, "And what is that?"

The Muslim replied, "When we go to Mecca, we at least find a coffin. But when you go to Jerusalem—your Mecca—you find nothing but an empty grave."

"That is just the difference," the missionary explained. "Mohammed is dead and in a coffin. But Christ has risen and all power in heaven and earth is given to Him. He is alive forevermore!"

Skeptics across the ages have attempted to explain away the resurrection of Jesus Christ. The first attempt is recorded in Matthew 28:11-15. At the insistence of the High Priests, Roman soldiers were posted at the tomb to be sure that the friends of Jesus did not secretly take His body away and claim that He had risen.

However, when the angels rolled the stone away and Jesus came forth from the grave, the soldiers went into the city and reported to the priests and elders of the Jews what had happened. The priests and elders bribed them with a large sum of money to say that while they slept His disciples had come and stolen the body away (Matthew 28:11-15).

The surest way to put this rumor to rest would have been to produce the body. But where was the body?

Jerusalem was a relatively small city. Surely the Jews and Romans could have found it. It couldn't have been carried very far in just a few hours. So why didn't they produce the body?

The fact is, within seven short weeks, the city of Jerusalem was seething with the preaching of the resurrection. The apostles were proclaiming it up and down every street of the city.

In a matter of weeks, those disciples were being imprisoned, persecuted, and even stoned for their preaching. Does it seem reasonable that these men would steal the dead body of Jesus, dispose of it, and then give their lives for a lie?

I have stood by the tomb of Lenin in Moscow, Russia. His embalmed body is still there, visible for the masses to view.

I have walked around in Westminster Abby and stood by the tombs of Britain's great men. Their bodies are buried there.

And I have walked around in what is believed to be the historical tomb of Jesus, but He is not there. HE IS RISEN! He is alive forevermore!

—4—

PNEUMATOLOGY:
The Doctrine of the Holy Spirit

Spiritual things are spiritually achieved and understood.

First Corinthians 2:14 says, "The man without the Spirit does not accept the things that come from the Spirit of God, for they are foolishness to him, and he cannot understand them, because they are spiritually discerned."

Therefore, an understanding of the person and work of the Holy Spirit is essential to know spiritual truth and to experience a relationship with the Lord Jesus Christ.

He said to them, "And I will ask the Father, and He will give you another Counselor to be with you forever" (John 14:16).

WHO IS THE HOLY SPIRIT?
Notice that I said "who" not "what." It greatly disturbs me to hear people refer to the Holy Spirit as "it." The Holy Spirit is a Person. He has all the attributes of "personhood":

- **Intelligence**—He knows things (1Corinthians 2:10-12). In fact, He is omniscient.
- **Will**—Scripture says He distributes Spiritual gifts "to each individual as He wills" (1 Corinthians 12:11).
- **Emotions**—He loves and grieves (Ephesians 4:30).

He hears, speaks, and guides (John 16:13). He teaches and stirs up memories (John 14:26), all functions performed only by a person.

The Holy Spirit is the Third Person of the Triune God. I readily acknowledge that the Trinity is difficult to defend logically (see Chapter 2), but it is a clear teaching of scripture. Divine attributes are ascribed to Him:

- Eternality (Hebrews 9:14)
- Omniscience (1Corinthians 2:10-12)
- Omnipotence (Micah 3:8)
- Omnipresence (Psalms 139:7)

He is equal in every way with the Father and with the Son. The Athanasian Creed, developed more than 1,500 years ago, states "such as the Father is, such is the Son, and such is the Holy Spirit."

When Jesus began to prepare His disciples for His approaching death, deep sadness and confusion gripped their hearts. Jesus promised them that after he was gone, he would send them another comforter. He said to them, "And I will ask the Father, and He will give you another Counselor to be with you forever" (John 14:16).

There are two Greeks words in the New Testament which are translated "another":

- "Heteros," meaning another of a different kind;
- And "allos" meaning another but of the same kind.

"Allos" is the word Jesus used to describe the other Helper which He promised. Incidentally, the Greek word for "helper" is "parakletos," which literally means one called along side to help.

In John 14:18, Jesus promised His disciples, "I will not leave you orphans; I will come to you."

Jesus promised that in the Person of the Holy Spirit He would be with them as their Helper, Comforter, Provider, and Enabler on His behalf forever.

WHERE DOES THE HOLY SPIRIT OPERATE?
It is important to note that the Holy Spirit has been active in the world since the beginning. He came in a special way at Pentecost, which we shall discuss later; but He has been active from the very beginning.

In Old Testament Times
To listen to some people talk about the Holy Spirit, you would think that the Holy Spirit was unknown and inactive before Pentecost.

The Hebrew word for spirit is "ruach." It appears as many as 370 times in the Old Testament, and as many as 30 of these refer positively to the third person of the Trinity—the Holy Spirit. Here are a few examples:

- In 1 Samuel 16, David was anointed the new king of Israel and the Holy Spirit came upon him. Then, years later, after he committed the sin of adultery and murder, and under deep conviction, he cried out, "Take not Thy Holy Spirit from me" (Psalm 51:11). As we shall see later, this is a prayer that a believer in Christ Jesus need never pray.

- The prophet Isaiah (see Isaiah 63:10-11) refers specifically to the Holy Spirit twice in this one reference.
- The Holy Spirit was an active agent in creation (see Genesis 1:1-2).
- Before Pentecost, the Holy Spirit came upon select individuals for special purposes and then in many cases left them. An example of this is King Saul (1Samuel 10:10; 11:6; 16:14). When he was anointed the first king of Israel the Holy Spirit came upon him; but after his disobedience to God the Holy Spirit departed from him.

In the Life of Jesus

The Holy Spirit was active in the life of Jesus in very special and specific ways:

- Scripture teaches us that He was active in His incarnation.
- Matthew 1:18 and Luke 1:35 reveal to us that the Holy Spirit came upon Mary in a miraculous way and she conceived the Lord Jesus while still a virgin.
- Matthew 3:16-17 says that when Jesus was baptized by John The Baptist, "heaven was opened, and he saw the Spirit of God descending like a dove and lighting on Him. And a voice from heaven said, 'This is my Son, whom I love; with him I am well pleased.'"
- He was active without measure in the ministry of Jesus while He was here on earth. John 3:34 says, "For the one whom God has sent speaks the words of God, for God gives the Spirit without limit."
- Luke 4:1 says, "Jesus, full of the Holy Spirit, returned from the Jordon and was led by the Spirit in the desert."

• He was at work at the resurrection of Jesus.
• And Romans 8:11 teaches us that it was the Holy Spirit that raised Him from the dead.

At Pentecost and Since Then

Something unique happened at Pentecost—a Jewish festival occurring 50 days after Passover. Thousands of Jews from all over the Roman Empire had come to Jerusalem for this festival.

While 120 disciples, including the apostles, were gathered in prayer, the Holy Spirit came upon them "and all of them were filled with the Holy Spirit and began to speak in other tongues as the Spirit enabled them" (Acts 2:4).

The prophet Joel prophesied that God would "pour out [His] Spirit on all people" (Joel 2:28). John the Baptist prophesied that Jesus would "baptize you with the Holy Spirit and with fire" (Matthew 3:11). At Pentecost, these prophesies were fulfilled and the Holy Spirit came into the world in a full, new way. In Old Testament times, the Holy Spirit came upon select people for specific purposes and in most cases left them when His purpose was completed.

In this, the church age, the Holy Spirit is in the world working within all people. This was a totally new concept for the Jews after Pentecost. Those first Christians—all Jews— were astonished when Peter revealed to them sometime later that the Holy Spirit had also come upon Gentile believers (Acts 11:12-18).

In the Life of the Spiritually Lost

Jesus said, "When He comes, He will convict the world of guilt in regard to sin and righteousness and judgment" (John 16:8).

The Holy Spirit convicts the world of sin, but what is sin? In Psalms 51, King David, pleading with God for His mercy after he had committed adultery and murder, uses three words to describe sin:

1. **Iniquity** – That is moral depravity and moral sickness.
2. **Transgression** – That is rebellion against the authority of God.
3. **Sin** - That is failure to measure up to the standard and expectations of God. My definition of sin is this: Anything that is contrary to or short of the will of God for one's life. The Holy Spirit convinces us of the reality of sin and our need for forgiveness and a Savior.

The Holy Spirit convicts the world of righteousness. God's standard of righteousness is Jesus Christ. Jesus said the Holy Spirit would convict of righteousness "because I go to my Father."

Therefore the only way to get to the Father is to have the righteousness of Christ, with which God fully clothes the believer, upon the believer's personal acceptance of and faith in Jesus as personal Savior (2 Corinthians 5:21).

This will be discussed in Chapter 5:

- **The Holy Spirit convicts of judgment.**
  Judgment—that which every person will be accountable for in his/her response to God—is a certainty. Scripture says that God has "set a day when he will judge the world with justice" (Acts 17:31), and that "just as a man is destined to die once, and after that to face judgment" (Hebrews 9:27).

• **The Holy Spirit draws the sinner to Christ.**
The Holy Spirit not only convicts the sinner of his need of a Savior, He also draws him or her under conviction to Jesus Christ. Scripture tells us that "no one can come to [Jesus] unless the Father who sent [Him] draws him..." (John 6:44). In the first place, a sinner would not be aware of his need of forgiveness if it were not for the work of the Holy Spirit. Perhaps the hardest words for a person to say are "I was wrong" or "I have sinned." Praise God for the work of the Holy Spirit who draws and leads us to Jesus!

In his book *Jesus Among Other Gods,* Ravi Zacharias tells the story about a girl who became hopelessly lost in a dark and dense forest.

The girl called and screamed but to no avail. Her alarmed parents and a group of volunteers frantically searched for her, but when darkness fell they had to give up for the night.

Early the next morning the girl's father reentered the forest to search for her and found her fast asleep on a rock. He called her name and ran to her. Startled awake, she threw her arms out to him. As he picked her up and hugged her, she repeated over and over again, "Daddy, I found you! Daddy, I found you."

She did not find her daddy; he found her. This is an imperfect illustration of what happens when a lost sinner comes to Christ. The Holy Spirit seeks him out, many times fast asleep to his lost condition, and leads him to the open arms of our Lord.

In the Life of the Believer
When a sinner responds to the conviction of the Holy Spirit,

repents of his sins, and places his faith in the Lord Jesus Christ, he is instantly "born again" by the Holy Spirit (John 3:3-8).

The Bible teaches that a sinner is dead in his or her trespasses and sins (Ephesians 2:1). A dead person needs life. And when a person places his faith in Christ he is made a new person.

"Therefore, if anyone is in Christ, he is a new creation; the old has gone, the new has come!" (2 Corinthians 5:17). The Holy Spirit takes up residence in the believer, giving the believer the opportunity for spiritual growth and maturity.

The Holy Spirit baptizes the believer into the spiritual body of Christ.

There is much confusion about the baptism of the Holy Spirit." This term does not occur in the English Bible. However, the baptism WITH the Holy Spirit came in fulfillment of John the Baptist's prophecy (Matthew 3:11) on the day of Pentecost (Acts 2:16-17).

At Pentecost, the Holy Spirit came in a full and unlimited way in the world and will continue His work until the Lord Jesus returns.

Every once in a while I hear someone pray, "Lord send Thy Holy Spirit." That is a prayer that is not necessary. The Holy Spirit IS here. He needs only for us to yield to His control.

Baptism BY the Holy Spirit happens to every believer the moment he places his faith in the Lord Jesus Christ as Savior. First Corinthians 12:13 says, "For we were all baptized by one Spirit into one body—whether Jews or Greeks, slave or free— and we were all given the one Spirit to drink.

> *The purpose of the sealing is to guarantee the security and certainty of the believer's salvation.*

THE BELIEVER IS SEALED IN THE HOLY SPIRIT

There are three passages that deal with the sealing of the Holy Spirit—2 Corinthians 1:21-22, Ephesians 1:13, and Ephesians 4:30.

Most conservative scholars believe that God the Father is the agent of the sealing and the Holy Spirit is the sphere in which the believer is sealed.

In his book, *The Holy* Spirit, Dr. Charles Ryrie states:

> *"When we say that something is sealed in wax, we mean that the substance of the seal is wax and that someone outside did the sealing. When the scriptures declare that the Christian is sealed with the Holy Spirit, they mean that He is the substance of the seal itself, and God is the outside person who does the sealing."*

The time of the sealing is the moment the believer receives Christ as Savior. Isn't it wonderful to know that we are sealed in the Holy Spirit and only God the Father has the authority and power of breaking that seal and He has promised never to do it?

The purpose of the sealing is to guarantee the security and certainty of the believer's salvation. The seal is guaranteed to keep us secure right up to the day we are received into heaven. Something that is sealed by God is as secure as the promises of God.

THE HOLY SPIRIT IS THE BELIEVER'S

...Teacher

When Jesus promised that He was going to send the Holy Spirit, He used the Greek word "parakletos" meaning "one sent along side to help" (John 16:7). In verse 13 of that chapter, He identifies the "parakletos" as the Spirit of truth and says that He will be our Teacher.

The Holy Spirit not only <u>inspired</u> the writing of Scripture; He <u>illumines</u> the Scripture. That is, He helps the believer to understand the spiritual truths the non-regenerated person cannot understand.

...Comforter

Jesus said to His disciples, when promising to send the Holy Spirit, "And I will pray the Father, and He shall give you another Comforter, that He may abide with you forever" (John 14:16 KJV).

A good example of this is when the Christian experiences the death of a loved one. The scripture says, "Brothers, we do not want you to be ignorant about those who fall asleep, or to grieve like the rest of men, who have no hope" (1 Thessalonians 4:13).

The Holy Spirit brings to our understanding the fact that Christian loved ones who die go immediately to be with the Lord. And He comforts us with the assurance that they are alive with Him and will one day be reunited with us in eternity. We are sorrowful that we have to lose those we love so dearly, but that sorrow is tempered with HOPE.

...Intercessor

Many times the Christian's problems are so complex that he

struggles to even know how to pray. In such instances, the Holy Spirit presents the deepest, unspeakable cries of our hearts before God, the Father.

The Apostle Paul tells us that "in the same way, the Spirit helps us in our weakness. We do not know what we ought to pray for, but the Spirit intercedes for us with groans that words cannot express" (Romans 8:26).

THE HOLY SPIRIT EMPOWERS THE BELIEVER

When a person, by faith, commits his life to Jesus Christ as Savior he is "born again" (John 3:3-8). He is given a new nature (2 Corinthians 5:17). The Apostle Peter describes this as a divine nature (2 Peter 1:4).

However, he still has the old nature and these two natures constantly war with each other (Galatians 5:13-26). The only way a person can have victory over the old nature is to "walk in the Spirit, and you shall not fulfill the lust of the flesh" (Galatians 5:16, NKJV).

What does that mean? It means living a life yielded to the control of the Holy Spirit. It means "being filled with the Holy Spirit."

I heard the story of a man visiting an old American Indian who had two dogs who were always fighting. The visitor asked the Indian, "Which one of these dogs wins? "

The Indian replied, "The one I feed."

The true believer has two natures: the old Adamic nature with which we are born. That is the nature to sin and rebel against God. And the new divine nature, which we receive when we accept Jesus Christ as Lord and Savior.

The nature we feed always wins. The victory comes when we, under the leadership and control of the Holy Spirit, feed upon the Word of God. The true believer, yielded to the control of the Holy Spirit, receives power to fulfill the commission our Lord has given to each believer.

The last words of Jesus to His followers before He ascended back to the Father were: "But you will receive power when the Holy Spirit comes on you; and you will be my witnesses in Jerusalem, and in all Judea and Samaria, and to the ends of the earth" (Acts 1:8).

There are many ways to be witnesses for our Lord: by the life we live, the example we set, the words we speak, the money we give, the friendship we show, and other ways. But, the effectiveness of these witnesses depends upon the power of the Holy Spirit working through it all.

Scripture teaches that all believers receive from the Holy Spirit "spiritual gifts." These gifts are not necessarily natural talents, but abilities endowed by the Holy Spirit to accomplish the purposes to which God has called us.

The purposes of these gifts are clearly spelled out for us in the scripture. They include equipping believers for the work of the ministry, edifying of the body of Christ (i.e. the Church), and bringing believers to Christian maturity and Christ-likeness (Ephesians 4:11-13).

5

ANTHROPOLOGY:
THE DOCTRINE OF MAN

The Psalmist, gazing out into uncluttered oriental skies, exclaimed:

> *"When I consider Your heavens,*
> *the work of Your fingers,*
> *the moon and the stars,*
> *which You have set in place,*
> *what is man that you are mindful of him,*
> *the son of man that you care for him?*
> —Psalm 8:3-4

Some people read this Psalm and conclude that when one compares the majesty, the magnitude, and the glory of the universe, man is not much. But that is exactly the opposite of what this scripture means.

The Psalmist observes that when we consider the magnitude of all that God has created, and the fact that He has created man just a little lower than the angels, man must be infinitely valuable and important.

A group of Greek philosophers were sitting around a table discussing what man is. Plato said, "Man is a two-legged animal." Socrates went out and brought a rooster and set him on the table and exclaimed, "Behold Plato's man."

The Crown of God's Creation

Man is unique. He is different and superior to everything else God created. He is the crown of God's creation. When one studies history and meditates upon the actions of mankind, it is hard to believe in the nobility of man.

During World War I, more that eight million people were killed. In World War II, 27 million military and 25 million civilians were killed. Murder, rape, child abuse, sexual assaults, robbery, political corruption, and countless other things tempt us to agree with Shopenhauer, who said, "Men are the devils of the earth."

So where do we get the idea of the nobility of man? We get it from the Bible in which God reveals His evaluation and purpose of man. We also see it demonstrated by countless millions who have lived godly, noble, sacrificial lives worshipping and serving God.

Man is the Direct Creation of God

At the beginning of time, God created man—male and female. I realize this statement is in direct conflict with the modern theory of evolution.

In my opinion, this theory is false for three reasons:

  1) It is contrary to scripture;
  2) It is illogical and irrational;
  3) And it is non-demonstrable.

It is asking too much of me to believe that man, in all his physical, emotional, and intellectual complexities, evolved from some microscopic speck of protoplasm! Man was created in the image of God (Genesis 1:27)—immortal and innocent.

Man has the capacity to understand moral truth—to distinguish between right and wrong. Scripture says that when God "...breathed into [man's] nostrils the breath of life, and the man became a living being" (Genesis 2:7).

Man has a body; he is a soul. The soul is the intellectual, emotional, and volitional aspect of a person's eternal being. He has a conscience with the ability to make moral choices and is, therefore, held responsible for his choices.

The Divine Purposes of Man
Simply stated, God's purposes for mankind are three-fold:

1) Fellowship with God and each other. Originally, mankind enjoyed a perfect relationship and fellowship with God. Sadly, that fellowship was broken by sin; but God "... demonstrates His own love for us in this: while we were still sinners, Christ died for us" (Romans 5:8), providing a way for that fellowship to be restored.
2) To rule over the earth. He was given the responsibility to dress and keep it. In general, mankind was to take care of God's earthly creation as an overseer, so to speak.
3) To be His partners in redemption. This does not mean that Christ's redemptive sacrifice is incomplete; the blood of Jesus Christ cleanses from all sin. He cried out from the cross, "It is finished" (John 19:30). Nothing can be or needs to be added to what Christ did in His death and resurrection! It means that He has given us the privilege of sharing the gospel of redemption with His world.

51

Jesus' last words to His disciples were: "But you will receive power when the Holy Spirit comes on you; and you will be my witnesses in Jerusalem, and in all Judea and Samaria, and to the ends of the earth" (Acts 1:8).

And the Apostle Paul cried out, "I want to know Christ and the power of His resurrection and the fellowship of sharing in his sufferings, becoming like him in his death..." (Philippians 3:10).

What did the apostle mean? He meant he had a deep desire to know Jesus Christ in a deeper, more profound way; He wanted to know, experientially, the power that raised Jesus from the dead, and share in whatever suffering and sacrifices that were necessary in bringing people into a saving relationship to Jesus Christ.

The word "fellowship" is a translation of the Greek word "koinonia." It means sharing in a common cause, or partnership in a cause.

He did not mean that the redemptive sacrifice of Christ was incomplete and therefore wanted to make up for what was lacking. Instead, he meant that he wanted the privilege to help make known the gospel of salvation in Christ, even though it may involve suffering. Incidentally, as a result of Paul's desire, it cost him his life.

The Christian is a partner with Jesus Christ in His redemptive cause. What a privilege and responsibility! What great satisfaction comes to one who is faithful in fulfilling this wonderful partnership; and, according to Jesus' word, bring glory to God: "This is to my Father's glory, that you bear much fruit, showing yourselves to be my disciples" (John 15:8).

These are the God-given responsibilities of man.

6

SOTERIOLOGY:
The Doctrine of Salvation

<u>Presuppositions</u>
To understand the doctrine of salvation, one must accept certain basic truths:

1) There is one eternal, holy, sovereign God
2) Man is responsible for his decisions and is accountable to God for his decisions and actions.

What do these propositions have to do with the biblical doctrine of salvation? Scripture reveals and experience confirms that mankind—from the time of Adam—has disobeyed God, rebelled against His authority, and broken fellowship with Him.

To restore this relationship and fellowship with God, we must have a Savior. Man was created to walk and talk—have a constant, unbroken relationship—with God; but rebellion separated us from Him.

The patriarch Job, struggling with this concept, cried out, "If only there were someone to arbitrate between us, to lay his hand upon us both…" (Job 9:33).

The Apostle Paul tells us that Jesus Christ is that mediator. First Timothy 2:5 says, "For there is one God and one mediator between God and men, the man Christ Jesus..."

Sinful man must have a savior—a mediator between himself and the Holy God to bridge the gap that separates us. That Man is Jesus Christ, sinful man's only Savior.

With this in mind, let us explore the subject of salvation.

The Meaning of Salvation

The word "saved" appears more than 50 times in the New Testament alone. And the word "salvation" appears at least 37 times.

Salvation is being saved from something—
the condemnation and punishment of sin.

SALVATION IS BEING SAVED
...From Something

The angel, announcing that the Virgin Mary would conceive of the Holy Spirit, said, "And she will bring forth a Son, and you shall call His name Jesus, for He will save His people from their sins" (Matthew 1:21).

The Bible states and experience confirms that "all have sinned and fall short of the glory of God..." (Romans 3:23). "Salvation" is being saved from the condemnation of sin. Sin, without exception, has consequences. One may get away with his sins in this life, but not in eternity.

People don't like to hear about hell these days—except as a curse word. Most preachers seldom preach about it. Many professed Christians, such as the cult called "Jehovah's Witnesses," deny the very existence of such a place.

But the Bible clearly teaches that there is a place called hell with "fire and brimstone" where the soul of the person who goes there never dies. See Jesus' teaching in Luke 16:19-31. Salvation is being saved from something—the condemnation and punishment of sin.

...To Something

Contrary to the ideas of millions of people who think the Christian life is a rigid formula of "do" and "don't" designed to rob us of pleasure and enjoyment, Jesus said, "...I have come that they may have life, and that they may have it more abundantly" (John 10:10).

The happiest, most joy-filled people I've ever known are committed Christians. Why wouldn't we be? We have been PARDONED from our sins; we have PEACE with God, ourselves, and others; and we have PURPOSE for which to live that gives excitement and fulfillment to life.

We are not only saved to an abundant life here and now, but we are also saved to eternal life with God. The soul of man never dies. For the Christian the soul goes immediately to be with God when the body dies.

Jesus said to the repentant thief on the cross, "Assuredly I say, today you will be with me in paradise" (Luke 23:39-43; see also 2 Corinthians 5:6-8). What a life that will be!

Just think: no more death, nor sorrow, nor tears, nor poverty, nor war, nor disappointment. We will enjoy eternal joy and fellowship with the Triune God, our Christian loved ones, and our brothers and sisters in Christ forever (see John 14:1-6 and Revelation 21:3-5).

Salvation is Described in the New Testament in 3 Ways:

- The believer has been saved from the "penalty" of sin. That's past tense.
- The believer is being saved from the "power" of sin. That's present tense.
- The believer will be saved from the "presence" of sin. That's future tense.

JUSTIFICATION (PAST TENSE)

This is a once-for-all experience in which God declares the repentant sinner righteous (Romans 4:22-24). When one honestly repents of (turns from) his sin and consciously places his faith in the crucified and resurrected Christ, Scripture teaches us that God gives to that person the very righteousness of Jesus Christ. Thereafter, God sees us through the righteousness of Christ which He imputes or attributes to the believer (Romans 4:1-5). Justification, then, is being declared righteous by God our Father.

SANCTIFICATION (PRESENT TENSE)

Sanctification is being made holy. The word holy in Scripture means "different" or "set apart." The believer is to be different from the world around him. He has been "separated to God" for God's purposes and glory. It is the lifestyle of growing spiritually in the likeness of Christ. This is a present struggle which every believer experiences. It is living under the control of the Holy Spirit, and therefore having victory over the power of sin.

GLORIFICATION (FUTURE TENSE)

Glorification is the consummation of salvation when the believer is delivered finally from every vestige of sin and made to conform to the image of the resurrected Christ.

"Beloved, now we are children of God; and it has not yet been revealed what we shall be, but we know that when He is revealed, we shall be like Him, for we shall see Him as He is. And everyone who has this hope in Him purifies himself, just as He is pure" (1 John 3:2-3).

Scripture teaches that when Jesus returns in all His glory, believers who are alive at the time will be instantly transformed and given a new body like the glorified body of the resurrected Christ. Those who have died will be resurrected and also given a glorified body (1Corinthians 15; 1Thessalonians 4:13-18).

How does one receive this salvation?
Notice I did not ask, "How does one *achieve* salvation?" We are told clearly in scripture that salvation is not the reward for good works.

SALVATION IS BY GRACE
Grace has been accurately defined as "the unmerited favor of God." It is God showing mercy when we deserved condemnation. It is the free, undeserved gift of God's forgiveness. Someone once said, "Grace is the unearned blessing of God to an unworthy recipient."

In Ashville, North Carolina, there's a house where Thomas Wolfe, the famous novelist, lived and worked. The desk and chair where he sat and wrote his famous novel, *You Can't Go Home Again,* has been preserved.

But Wolfe was wrong. Jesus Christ has paved the way back home to the Father. Because of what our Savior has done, the Father welcomes us back home.

Scripture says, "For by grace you have been saved through faith, and that not of yourselves; it is the gift of God, not of works, lest anyone should boast" (Ephesians 2:8-9). And "the wages of sin is death, but the gift of God is eternal life in Christ Jesus our Lord" (Romans 6:23).

This grace—this free gift—is not cheap. It cost Jesus Christ His death on the cross. The Bible says, "The soul who sins shall die" (Ezekiel 18:4).

When Jesus died on the cross He took our sin upon Himself and died in our place. He paid the penalty for the sin of every person who receives Him in repentance and faith.

Scripture teaches us that God made Jesus "...who knew no sin to be sin for us, that we might become the righteousness of God in Him" (2 Corinthians 5:20-21; Isaiah 53:4-6). And the Apostle Paul gives us the wonderful news that, "God demonstrates His own love toward us, in that while we were still sinners, Christ died for us" (Romans 5:8).

One poet so eloquently sings it:

> *"There was none other good enough to pay the price of sin;*
> *He only could unlock the gates of heaven and let us in. O,*
> *can it be that on the tree the Savior died for me?*
> *My soul is thrilled, my heart is filled to think He died*
> *for me."*

We must not forget that sin is not only transgression of the law and will of God; it is also failure to measure up to God's standard.

I was in an evangelistic crusade in Japan in 1965. One day, I was invited to attend the city council meeting in the city where I was preaching. After the meeting was over, the mayor said to me, "Pastor, last night my son asked me a question I could not answer. I don't want to lose face with my son. Can you help me?"

The question was, "Father, what is the difference between Buddhism and Christianity?"

I hesitated for a moment and prayed silently for wisdom, and then said to him, "Your honor, most all religions have some good and offer some reward if one lives up to their teachings; but only Jesus Christ makes provision for FAILURE."

Jesus' death not only pays the penalty for our sin; His righteousness given to us makes up for our failure. The believer will stand in the presence of God COMPLETE, lacking nothing, because the righteousness of Christ becomes ours through faith.

> ***Grace has been accurately defined as***
> ***"the unmerited favor of God."***

SALVATION IS THROUGH FAITH

This "grace gift" must be asked for and received by faith. Faith is trust. It is confidence in the validity of God's promise, and the sufficiency of the atoning death and resurrection of Jesus Christ. One must confess that he is a sinner without excuse. He must believe that Jesus died for him and paid in full the penalty of his sin. He must have confidence that Jesus wants to save, and that He is able to save.

Dr. William Newell, the renowned professor at Moody Bible Institute put it this way:

"O, the love that drew salvations plan!
O, the grace that brought it down to man!
O, the mighty gulf that God did span,
At Calvary."

Hallelujah! What a Savior! What a life we have in Him right now, and better still, what an eternal future we will have with Him!

7

ECCLESIOLOGY:
THE DOCTRINE OF THE CHURCH

True churches are God's redemptive instrument in society.

God gave us three institutions:

1) The Family
2) Government
3) The Church

I believe true churches are God's redemptive instrument in society. Elton Trueblood once said, "...the church of Jesus Christ is meant to be a redemptive fellowship, in the sense that it is trying to save, not itself, but the world."

If this is true, and I believe it is, then it is extremely important that we understand the nature and purposes of the church. The church has a unique role to play in society. It alone has the responsibility of fulfilling the commission our Lord, who founded the church, has given to it.

The Nature of the Church
The Greek word "ekklesia" translated "church" in the New

Testament, is a combination of two words, *ek* meaning *out* and *kaleo* meaning *to call.* "Church" is rightfully translated in this the New Testament context as *the called out ones.* The church is made up of those who have placed their faith in Jesus Christ as Savior and have been called out to be His people.

The Church is a Living Organism

Many places in the Bible call it the "Body of Christ" (Ephesians 1:22-23; 4:4, 12, 16; 5:23; Colossians 1:18, 24). This spiritual body is made up of born again believers. Jesus said you must be born again (see John 3:3).

What does this mean? It means that when a person repents, or turns from, his sin and places his faith in Jesus Christ, he becomes a new person. He is made a child of God. He is spiritually born into the Kingdom of God. This is happening to people in every part of the world. In this sense it is universal and invisible. Every true believer is baptized by the Holy Spirit into Jesus Christ the moment he places his faith in Him (1 Corinthians 12:13).

The Church is a Dynamic Local Fellowship

The word "church" appears in the New Testament at least 110 times. Ninety-five of these refer to a local church. Christians in a local area come together and organize themselves into a church to fulfill the purposes for which Christ instituted His church.

It is important at this point to understand that every genuine believer in Jesus Christ is a member of the universal church. However, every member of the local church is not necessarily a member of the universal church. A person may choose, for various reasons, to join a local church without having a genuine faith in or commitment to Jesus Christ as his personal Savior and Lord.

A good example of this was revealed in a long article in the Houston Chronicle on March 18, 2006, written by an open, publicly professed atheist who had joined a local church for political reasons. However, the Bible is very clear that only people who have, themselves, repented of their sins and in faith committed themselves to Jesus Christ as personal Savior, are members of the true church.

The Purposes of the Church
It is very important not only that we know WHO we are but WHY we are. We can know we are succeeding only if we know what we are to be doing. Someone correctly said, "If you don't know where you are going any old road will get you there."

Our Lord Jesus Christ has spelled out His plan and purposes for the church very clearly. He has chosen the church to fulfill His redemptive ministry in the world which is a very unique calling:

- Science may tell us the distance from the earth to the sun. It is left to the church to tell sinners how far they are from the Son.
- Astronomers may tell us the movements and ways of the stars. It is left to the church to tell men the way to God.
- Geologists may tell us the ages of rocks. It is left to the church to tell us of the Rock of Ages.
- Sociologists may tell us how to put a new coat on every man. It is left to the church to tell us how to put a new man in the coat.
- Psychologists may tell us how to have peace of mind. It is left to the church to tell us how to have peace with God.

- Economists may tell us how to lift living standards. It is left to the church to lift moral and spiritual standards.
- Civic Clubs may show us how to have friendship with men. It is left to the church to show us how to be friends with God.

The local church has three basic purposes:

1) Worship
2) Evangelism
3) Fellowship and Edification of the believer

WORSHIP

The first, and most important purpose of the church is the worship of the Triune God. Jesus taught us that God is Spirit and He seeks people who will worship Him in Spirit and Truth (John 4:23).

Worship is recognizing the "worthship" of God in Christ. It is humbling oneself in His presence and confessing His worthiness to receive worship. The Psalmist said, "I will call upon the Lord, who is worthy to be praised" (Psalm 18:3).

Worship is not entertainment. It is not seeking a blessing. It is blessing God! It is recognizing His Majesty and Glory and Holiness.

The disciples came to Jesus on one occasion and asked Him to teach them to pray. Prayer itself is to begin in worship. Jesus taught us to pray: "Our Father in heaven, hallowed by Thy Name…" (Matthew 6:9).

His Name and His person is to be exalted and held in reverence. Jesus Christ is God Incarnate. Jesus is to be worshiped and praised. The Bible says:

> *"Therefore God exalted him to the highest place and gave him the name that is above every name, that at the name of Jesus every knee should bow, in heaven and on earth and under the earth, and every tongue confess that Jesus Christ is Lord, to the glory of God the Father."*
> —Philippians 2:9-11

...Worship is PRAISE

It is an act of expressing praise for His glory, majesty, power, holiness, and perfect righteousness. It is praising Him to others that they too may come to appreciate who He is and worship Him as well.

...Worship is THANKSGIVING

It is giving thanks for His goodness, love, salvation, sacrificial death, and triumphant resurrection. It is giving thanks for the forgiveness of sin and His assurance that we, too, will be like Him (Romans 8:28-29; 1 John 3:2).

...Worship is PRIVATE and PUBLIC

Some of the greatest worship experiences of my life have taken place when I was all alone. Years ago while visiting our daughter and family in California, I received a phone call that my father, in a hospital in Lufkin, Texas, was near death having suffered a heart attack.

I had gotten just a few hours sleep after an overnight flight from Houston. But, I went to the airport and arrived back in Houston about 9:00 p.m., got in my car, and started the two hour drive to Lufkin. Few times have I felt the presence of God more powerfully than I did that night.

Driving in a part of the state where I grew up in poverty and privation, and thinking about how the Lord had worked in my life, I found myself singing something I had never heard before: "I sought for a way just to praise Him. I sought for a way just to magnify His Name. I sought for a way to exalt the Name of Jesus for the things He has done for me."

Worship can and should be practiced privately.

The Bible emphasizes the importance of public, corporate worship. Hebrews 10:25 says, "Let us not give up meeting together, as some are in the habit of doing, but let us encourage one another—and all the more as you see the Day approaching."

There is something physically, emotionally, and spiritually therapeutic about public worship. The leadership of the church has a profound responsibility to teach people how, and lead the people in true, Spirit-filled corporate worship.

EVANGELISM
The church is commissioned to "make disciples." That is, we are commanded to share the gospel of Jesus Christ to the ends of the earth, beginning in our own home. We are commissioned to expand the Kingdom of God.

From its very beginning, the church has been criticized and persecuted for their efforts in evangelism. Millions of Christians have been martyred because of their efforts of evangelism; yet to be true to our Lord we must not fail here.

One historian in another century said, "The blood of the martyrs is the seed of the Church." In fact the very word "witness" is a translation of the Greek word "martures," from which we get our word "martyr."

Recently, I was listening to a service on Christian Radio. Dr. Ed Young, the renowned pastor of the Second Baptist Church in Houston, Texas, quoted from the diary of a young Christian martyr in Africa:

> *"I am part of the fellowship of the Unashamed. The die is cast. I've stepped over the line. The decision has been made. I am a Disciple of Jesus Christ. I will not look back, let up, slow down, back away, or be still. My past is redeemed. My present makes sense. My future is secure. I am finished and done with low living, sight walking, smooth knees, colorless dreams, tamed visions, worldly talking, weak giving, and dwarfed goals. My face is set. My gait is fast. My goal is heaven. My road is narrow. My way is rough. My companions are few. My Guide is reliable. My mission is clear. I will not give up, shut up, let up, until I have stayed up, prayed up, stored up, and paid up for the cause of Jesus Christ. I must go 'til He comes, give 'til I drop, preach 'til everyone knows, and work 'til He stops me. And when He comes for His own, He will have no problem recognizing me because my banner will be flying high."*

To be true to our calling, we must share the gospel of our Lord Jesus Christ regardless of the cost!

The word "gospel" means "good news." It is the good news that Jesus Christ is the Savior from sin and its guilt and penalty. First John 1:9 says that "if we confess our sins, he is faithful and just and will forgive us our sins and purify us from all unrighteousness."

We have a good message! Christians have a duty to be faithful to see that this message of good news is shared with as many people as possible—to the ends of the earth!

Dr. Peter Kuzmic, president of the Evangelical Seminary in Croatia, tells of a phone call he received from the chief editor of a daily newspaper with the largest circulation in his country.

He had once been a committed communist; but had come to see the fallacy of the basic principles and world view of communism. He was now equally pro-active in the pro-democracy movement. He asked Dr. Kuzmic to write a full-page article for the Sunday edition of his paper relating to the Ten Commandments.

In the conversation with Dr. Kuzmic, he said,

> *"We (communists) had high ideals, lofty goals. ... For the last few years we have been trying to force a roof on this new construction, and now this whole project has collapsed and it caved in because it didn't have any foundation. We dare not have another failing experiment now that democracy has arrived."*

His final sentence was a missionary challenge:

> *"This is too important for the world; this is too important for democracy; and this is too important for the new society. Please don't keep it locked up within the four walls of your churches and your theological classrooms."*

Evangelism is essential, not only to the fulfillment of our Lord's commission; it is also essential to any free and civil society. But society will not be changed simply by adding members to the church; therefore, the church must not become like the world in order to get more members.

The message, program, and mission of the church must not be determined by exit polls! Our purpose is to change the world, not become like it. We must not fail. Too much depends upon it!

Church historian Martin Marty, wrote in the August 9, 1993 edition of Newsweek magazine regarding the decline of mainline churches:

> *"To give the whole store away to match what this year's market says the unchurched want is to have the people who know the least about faith determine most about its expression. The mainline denominations may be dying because they lost their theological integrity."*

EDIFICATION

The church not only has the responsibility of "making disciples" but also of "maturing" disciples. The church's purpose is to:

- Make disciples – Win or love and lead people to faith in Jesus Christ as Savior.
- Mark disciples – Baptize them in the Name of the Father, and of the Son, and of the Holy Spirit.
- Mature disciples – Teach them to observe everything our Lord has taught us.

Edification is to be done on many levels: in the home; teach our children; and from the pulpit. Pastors should be expositors of the Word of God.

It is to be done in Bible study classes at church and other places such as small groups, Bible conferences, Bible schools, seminaries, and wherever it is effective to do so.

We are to teach what the Bible says and what the Bible means and how to apply it to all of life's situations and circumstances.

The Church is to teach Christian doctrines and ethics. It is to help each other discover and develop their Spiritual gifts. It is to train believers how to witness, how to pray, how to be and do all that our Lord has commanded us.

The question comes, "How can we do these noble things effectively?" We are weak. We live in a house of flesh, pulled and pushed by a carnal, wicked world. At times, we meet resistance from the very ones to whom we are called to witness. How can we achieve the purposes for which we are called and commissioned?

Our Lord uses four strategies to channel His power to and through us:

1) The Gospel (Romans 1:16; Hebrews 4:12,13)
   The Bible says "it is the power of God to salvation for everyone who believes." As we have said, the gospel is the good news that Jesus died to pay our sin debt. He rose from the grave to give us eternal life. There is something awesome about the gospel, especially when shared in love and through a loving and holy life.

2) A Holy Life
   "For God did not call us to uncleanness, but to holiness" (1 Thessalonians 4:7), so "let your light so shine before men, that they may see your good works and glorify your Father in heaven" (Matthew 5:16). The shame of the church is the unholy lives of too many of its members. The glory of the church is the holiness and consistent living of so many.

I have preached the gospel many times and many places in the former Soviet Union. As you remember, under communism children were not allowed to be taught about Christ and His redemption. A person under the age of 18 was not allowed to be a member of a church. They were constantly brainwashed by atheistic communism.

A Christian teenager who grew up in this environment was asked what most influenced him to be a Christian. His answer: "The holy lives of my parents." A holy life, lived in love and compassionate ministry, has a power that will not be ignored. When the gospel is shared through a loving, holy life, the world will listen with respect.

3) The Holy Spirit

"For our gospel did not come to you in word only, but also in power, and in the Holy Spirit..." (1 Thessolonians 1:5; see also John 16:7-11; Acts 1:8).

The Holy Spirit, the Third Person of the Holy Trinity, gives power for holy living. He anoints the holy life with Spiritual power in witness and gives boldness to share the gospel. He convicts the unbeliever of his sin and need of a Savior; and when the person under conviction turns to Christ in repentance and faith He regenerates that person, transforming him/her into a believer and baptizes him/her into the spiritual body of Christ. Without the power of the Holy Spirit no person regardless of his persuasive powers can lead a person to Christ. Only the Holy Spirit has that power.

4) Prayer

"...men always ought to pray and not lose heart" (Luke 18:1). "When they had prayed...they spoke the word of God with boldness...And with great power the apostles gave witness to the resurrection of the Lord Jesus, and great grace was upon them all" (Acts 4:31-33).

Prayer invites God into the situation. Prayer lets loose the power of God AND the resources of God into a believer's life, relationships, and circumstances. When these early believers prayed they were filled afresh with the Holy Spirit, they were filled with boldness to speak, and they were filled with the love of Christ that motivated their sharing.

These four strategies are inter-related and cannot be separated successfully. The gospel must be channeled through a holy life and anointed and empowered by the Holy Spirit. Prayer activates the Holy Spirit to strengthen the believer in his daily life and witness and energizes the gospel which is shared and makes worship a warm, transforming experience with God.

Prayer lets loose the power of God AND the resources of God into a believer's life, relationships, and circumstances.

The Ordinances of the Church

The New Testament reveals and describes two ordinances of the church: Baptism and the Lord's Supper. Both of these ordinances symbolize what our Lord has done to redeem us from sin, the new life the believer has in Him, and the hope we have for the future.

We use the word "ordinance" instead of the word sacrament because sacrament conveys the idea that baptism and the Lord's Supper have saving power. Such a notion is not what the New Testament teaches.

The English word ordinance is derived from the Latin word "ordinare," which means "to set in order," something being authoritatively ordained. When applied to baptism and the Lord's Supper it means they are sacred and symbolic acts divinely instituted (see Matthew 28:19-20; 1 Corinthians 11:24).

BAPTISM

Baptism is the immersion of a believer in water as a public confession of his faith in the death, burial, and resurrection of the Lord Jesus Christ, and a testimony of the new life Christ has given to him.

In the New Testament, baptism is always administered to a believer—to someone who has understood and received the forgiveness offered through Christ's substitutionary death on the cross repenting of their sins.

There are no accounts of infant baptism in the New Testament. Infant baptism grew out of the heretical (unbiblical) doctrine of "Baptismal Regeneration." That was the teaching that original sin is washed away by baptism and the person is thereby regenerated, made a new person, and saved.

Roman Catholicism teaches that an infant who dies without being baptized is not allowed into heaven; rather the child goes to "limbo," a place similar to heaven but separated from the presence of God. A place like "limbo" is totally foreign to the New Testament.

It was the doctrine of baptismal regeneration that eventually led to changing the "mode" of baptism. Any competent scholar of Greek (the language in which the New Testament was written) will agree that the mode of baptism was by immersion.

The Greek word translated baptism is "baptizo," which means to dip, or plunge under water, or immerse in water. It is unfortunate that the translators of the New Testament into English did not translate the word "baptize." Instead, they "transliterated" it. That is, they simply substituted English letters for the Greek letters and created the word "baptize."

The mode of baptism was changed for convenience. It was difficult to immerse an infant, or a critically ill adult; but, according to the doctrine of baptismal regeneration, they must be baptized in order to be saved. This "inconvenience" gradually led to sprinkling as baptism.

Baptism is a symbol of one's faith in the death, burial, and resurrection of Jesus Christ and a testimony of his or her new life in Christ. When one is immersed in water, he is confessing his faith in the death and burial of Jesus Christ. When he rises from the water, he is confessing faith in His resurrection (see Romans 6:3-5).

It is an act of loving obedience to the command of our Lord. It is the act whereby a believer is admitted into the fellowship in a local church.

THE LORD'S SUPPER

On the evening before our Lord was crucified, He gathered with His disciples to observe the Passover Feast—the most solemn feast of the Jews. This feast commemorated the grand and awesome deliverance of the Jews from Egyptian slavery.

After the feast, Jesus took bread, broke it, gave it to His disciples, and said, "This is my body given for you; do this in remembrance of me" (Luke 22:19). Likewise, He took the cup saying, "This cup is the new covenant in My blood, which is poured out for you" (Luke 22:20).

The ordinance of the Lord's Supper, or communion, was intended to be a most solemn experience when a Christian, in a very tangible way, keeps alive and pays homage to the sacrificial crucifixion of our Lord. Yet it may be the most misunderstood and abused of all Christian doctrines and practices. Let's evaluate some of those misunderstandings:

Transubstantiation

The Roman Catholic theory of the Lord's Supper is known as transubstantiation, which teaches that the bread and wine, when consecrated by the priest, become the actual body and actual blood of Jesus Christ. When one eats the bread and drinks the wine, he is eating and drinking the body and blood of Jesus Christ.

It is obvious these were not the literal body and blood of Jesus for He sat with his disciples very much alive in His body. Dr. W. A. Criswell writes:

> *"Not only does such a view (transubstantiation) savor of cannibalism, it denies the finality and completeness of the sacrifice of Christ on the cross (Hebrews 9:28). The bread and wine were symbols of His broken body and shed blood. These ordinances were to be observed "in remembrance of Me."*

Consubstatiation

This is the doctrine set forth by Martin Luther. He rejected the Roman Catholic doctrine of transubstantiation and advocated the theory that the invisible and mystical presence of Christ is present "in, with, and under" the elements when the believer partakes of the bread and wine.

Memorial Supper

The Lord's Supper was a memorial supper, nothing more and nothing less. Jesus said to "...do this in remembrance of Me" (Luke 22:19). The Apostle Paul, in 1 Corinthians 11:23-29, gives the most complete statement concerning the Lord's Supper:

> *"For I received from the Lord what I also passed on to you: The Lord Jesus, on the night he was betrayed, took bread,*

and when he had given thanks, he broke it and said, 'This is my body, which is for you; do this in remembrance of me.' In the same way, after supper he took the cup, saying, 'This cup is the new covenant in my blood; do this, whenever you drink it, in remembrance of me.' For whenever you eat this bread and drink this cup, you proclaim the Lord's death until he comes.

Therefore, whoever eats the bread or drinks the cup of the Lord in an unworthy manner will be guilty of sinning against the body and blood of the Lord. A man ought to examine himself before he eats of the bread and drinks of the cup. For anyone who eats and drinks without recognizing the body of the Lord eats and drinks judgment on himself."

Memory is tremendously important! Taking the Lord's Supper is not something we do to gain favor with God; it is something we do to keep alive the memory of what the Lord Jesus Christ did for us to make us acceptable with a holy God. Jesus gave us the supper "lest we forget!"

When believers come together to take of the supper they are, in a visible way, calling into memory that awesome experience of our Lord when He was crucified as a perfect, adequate, substitutionary sacrifice for our sins.

The Governance of the Local Church
As I have stated earlier, 95 of more than 110 times the word "ekklesia" (church) appears in the New Testament it refers to the local church.

The New Testament knows nothing of an ecclesiastic authority. Churches in the New Testament were local, independent, autonomous bodies of believers. The only outside authority recognized by the local churches was the authority of the apostles, whose teachings were binding.

When one reads the New Testament it is obvious that the government of the churches was in the hands of all the members, not in the hands of an authoritarian group.

THE LOCAL CHURCH IS A CHRISTOCRACY

Christ is the head of the church. "And God placed all things under his feet and appointed him to be head over everything for the church, which is his body..." (Ephesians 1:22-23; see also Ephesians 4:15-16 and Colossians 1:18).

Many times we hear people say, "The church is a democracy." That is true to a certain extent. It is the responsibility of the church to discover the mind of Christ in all it seeks to do and to govern itself under His Lordship.

But when members of a church are committed to the Lordship of Christ and His perfect will for the church, the Holy Spirit will lead that church to know and do His will in unity and love. All that they are and do will fall in line with the teachings of Christ and the Apostles.

The local church, ultimately, must make the final decisions concerning its governance, organization, and mission. However, it must always follow what they believe to be the will of Christ Who is the head of the church.

THE OFFICERS OF THE CHURCH

The New Testament sets forth two officers (or offices) of the church: Pastors and Deacons.

Pastors

Scripture uses three terms to describe men whom most evangelical churches call "Pastor."

In Acts 20 we find the Apostle Paul on his way to Jerusalem where he would be arrested and imprisoned. While anchored at the port city of Miletus, he sent messengers to Ephesus and called for the elders of the church to meet with him at Miletus. In this meeting he used three terms to describe these men and their responsibilities:

1) **Elder** – This is an English translation of the Greek word "presbuteros" (Acts 20:17).
2) **Bishop or Overseer** – From the Greek term "episcopos" (Acts 20:28).
3) **Pastor or shepherd** – From the Greek term "poimein" (Acts 20:28).

The elders are to be bishops overseeing the work of the church and lead it to fulfill its mission. They are to "guard the souls" of the members (Acts 20:28; Hebrews 13:17) from false doctrines and teach them to mimic the Great Shepherd.

They are to shepherd, or pastor the people by teaching them, feeding them spiritually, and protecting them from internal attacks. A friend of mine said to me, "God doesn't call men to be cowboys. He calls them to be shepherds. A cowboy drives the herd. A shepherd leads the flock."

Pastors or elders are to teach and train the members to minister to the needs of each other, and to witness to and lead lost people to the Savior. A church may have many pastors, depending upon the size of the church, but typically it has only one Senior Pastor.

As a pastor for more than 40 years, I can say that the responsibilities of a sincere and conscientious pastor carry greater burdens than any other position a man could have. They are eternal in their implications. I can also say, looking back and now knowing and having experienced all I have, if I had my life to live over again I would still want to spend it as pastor of one of our Lord's churches.

Assuming that the pastor is a godly, Spirit-filled man, true to the Word of God, and true to the principles delineated above, churches have tremendous responsibilities to their pastors. They are to remember him in prayer (Hebrews 13:7) and respect him (1 Thessalonians 5:12-13; 1 Timothy 5:17-20).

I have problems with people calling their pastor by his first name—especially from the platform in a worship service. I am 30 years older than my pastor, but I never call him by his first name. I call him "pastor." I have that kind of respect for him.

The church also has the responsibility of supporting the pastors financially. I heard the story of a man listening to his pastor praying for the poor and the humble. The man prayed, "Lord, you keep him humble and we'll keep him poor." As a whole, churches are doing a better job now than in years past.

Hebrews 13:17 also says that the church is to obey the pastor. This is another way of saying they are to obey the spiritual truths he teaches and cooperate with him as he leads the church to fulfill its mission.

Deacons
The word "deacon" is a translation of the Greek word "diakonos," which means a servant. A deacon, then, is one

who serves or ministers to others. Jesus called Himself a "minister" ("diakonos"; Matthew 20:28).

The Bible gives no incident in which deacons are a ruling or executive board. The first deacons were chosen to minister to Grecian widows within the church (Acts 6: 1-7).

They are partners with the pastor in ministry. They are partners with the pastor in discovering the will of God for the church, and leading the church to fulfill the will of God for the church. And they are to be peacemakers within the church body (Acts 6:1-7).

In the first church, there arose a disturbance concerning the benevolent ministry of the church to "Grecian widows," or widows of the Hellenistic Jews. This may have been the first time the church was accused of discrimination.

The apostles asked the church to choose seven men to be responsible for this ministry, and they were to be peacemakers in the fellowship of that first church. It's interesting to note that other than the passage in Acts 6, the Bible does not spell out a job description of deacon.

It is also significant that these men were chosen by the church, not by the apostles. This was not the beginning of an ecclesiastical hierarchy.

THE SUPPORT OF THE CHURCH

When one understands the world-wide mission of the church the question naturally comes, "How do we finance such an awesome task?" The Bible is crystal clear: tithes and offerings.

What is the tithe? It is one-tenth of one's income. Someone once said, "Tithing is an Old Testament teaching. We are no longer under the law."

So should a Christian under the grace of God give less than a Jew give under law?

Also, the New Testament teaches, "On the first day of the week let each one of you lay something aside, storing up as he may prosper, that there be no collections when I come" (1 Corinthians 16:2). "Offerings" are money and goods given over and above the tithe given to advance the total mission of the church.

I testify from more than 65 years of experience that God keeps His promise made in Malachi 3:10. He blesses those who practice tithing from a loving and compassionate heart.

Let Christ Jesus be glorified in the churches! Let there be love expressed in unity as we strive to fulfill the mission our Lord has given to his churches.

8

ESCHATOLOGY:
The Doctrine of Last Things

Eschatology, a word derived from the Greek "eschatos," is the doctrine of last things. It is a study of events that will unfold during the closing days of human history as we have known it. It includes the study of the return of Jesus Christ to the earth, the resurrection of the dead, and the ushering in of the eternal Kingdom of God.

It should also include a discussion of what happens to a person who dies before the return of our Lord. Let us look at this ultra important question before we deal with the end times.

Where one spends eternity depends on what he does with Jesus Christ during his lifetime.

The Immortality of Mankind
The Bible states that when God created man He breathed into His nostrils the breath of life and man became a living soul. The soul of a person never dies, and the Bible teaches that when a person physically dies his soul goes immediately to one of two places: heaven or hell (see Luke 16:19-31).

Where one spends eternity depends on what he does with Jesus Christ during his lifetime. To the surprise of many, there will be no judgment in the future to determine one's eternal destiny. God judged sin in Christ on Calvary's cross. We can either accept Him and live eternally, or reject Him and what He did on the cross and pay our own sin's debt forever. That decision must be made in one's lifetime.

What Happens to a Christian at Death?

The greatest example of faith in the New Testament is that of the repentant thief, crucified with Jesus. He had no outward evidence of the deity of Jesus. Everything about that scene was a picture of failure.

But when he turned to Jesus and said, "Remember me when you come into your kingdom" (Luke 23:42).

Jesus responded, "Assuredly I say to you, today you shall be with me in paradise" (Luke 23:43).

The Apostle Paul made it crystal clear that when a Christian dies, he or she goes immediately to be with our Lord and Savior Jesus Christ. The great Apostle, under the inspiration of the Holy Spirit, said, "...to be absent from the body is to be present with the Lord" (2 Corinthians 5:1-9).

In the historic battle for Jerusalem, when Jews were fighting to re-establish the nation of Israel for the first time in centuries, Colonel David Marcos, a West Point trained officer, was killed. In his pocket was found the following by an anonymous writer:

I am standing upon the seashore. A ship at my side spreads her white sails to the morning breeze and starts for the blue ocean.

She is an object of beauty and strength—and I stand and watch her, until at length she hangs like a speck of while cloud, just where the sea and sky come and meet each other.

Then someone at my side says, "There, she is gone."

Gone where? Gone from my sight is all. She is just as large in mast and hull and spar as she was when she left my side, and just as able to bear her load of living weights to its place of destination.

Her diminished size is in me, not in her; and just as someone by my side says, "There, she is gone", on that distant shore there are other eyes watching for her coming, ready to take up the glad shout, "Here she comes." And such is dying.

And I say such is dying "in the Lord." When a Christian dies, the moment the soul leaves the body our Lord and millions who have gone on before us, watching over the portals of glory shout, "Here he or she comes! Welcome home!"

Jesus said to His sorrowing disciples, "I am going to prepare a place for you. And if I go and prepare a place for you, I will come back and take you to be with me that you also may be where I am" (John 14:2-4). Let's examine that passage.

Heaven is a Real Place
The Book of Revelation describes the place that Jesus mentioned in the passage above. The capital city, the New Jerusalem, is a cube of 1500 x 1500 x 1500 miles. It's a rather large city, don't you think?

It is a place of pristine beauty far beyond the ability of human languages and imagination to describe. There is no death, sickness, sorrow, tears, hate, or crime—only joy indescribable and full of glory. What a place!

Heaven is a Place of Unbroken Fellowship

The Triune God is there. Jesus said, "You also may be where I am." The Revelator said, "Behold the dwelling place of God is with men, and He will dwell with them, and they shall be His people. God Himself will be with them and be their God" (Revelation 21:3).

What an unimaginable experience it will be to fall before Jesus and bathe His nail-scared feet with our tears of gratitude! We have felt His touch spiritually; but what a thrill it will be to feel the touch of the nail-scarred hand!

Fellowship with those gone on before will be revived in a perfect, untarnished way. Yes, we will know each other in heaven.

Dr. G. Campbell Morgan, a renowned London pastor, tells of the time he stood next to his father after he finished preaching the morning worship service. A good woman came to his father and asked, "Pastor, do you expect to know your loved ones in heaven?"

His father responded, rather brusquely, "My good woman, do you expect I shall be a bigger fool in heaven than here?"

Scripture says "We will know even as we are known." What a wonderful, exhilarating thought!

One day Jesus will return in great glory and universal victory, and HE won't be late!

CERTAINTY OF THE SECOND COMING OF JESUS

Nothing is more clearly taught in the New Testament than the personal, glorious, visible return of our Lord Jesus Christ to this earth. Jesus told His disciples, "I am going to prepare a place for you. And if I go and prepare a place for you, I will come back and take you to be with me that you also may be where I am" (John 14:2-4).

Weeks after His glorious resurrection, while His followers marveled at His ascension, two angels appeared to them and said, "This same Jesus, who has been taken from you into heaven, will come back in the same way you have seen him go into heaven" (Acts 1:11).

Yet, millions of scoffers mock the idea that He will return. This should not surprise us. The Apostle Peter prophesied, "...you must understand that in the last days scoffers will come, scoffing and following their own evil desires" (2 Peter 3:3).

Many liberal theologians and ministers ridicule the idea. Don't let that cause you to despair. In one of the Messianic Psalms we are told that, "The One enthroned in heaven laughs; the Lord scoffs at them" (Psalm 2:4).

There is an old saying, "He who laughs last, laughs longest." The skeptics and cynics may "conspire and...plot in vain" (Psalm 2:1), but that changes nothing. Scripture clearly teaches that He shall return visibly and victoriously to reign, as the old hymn states, "where'er the sun does its successive journeys run," and "every eye will see Him, even they who pierced Him" (Zechariah 12:10; John 19:37).

In my earlier years, I wondered how every eye would see Him as He returns to the earth. But my curiosity disappeared one day in the early 1960s, as I sat in my living room watching the televised "splashdown" of our first astronaut into space.

If modern technology can show to the whole earth an event that took place in one small place in the Pacific Ocean, then surely the eternal, all-powerful God can make the return of Jesus Christ visible to the whole universe!

Many sensationalists have predicted dates when He will return. As an example, the Jehovah's Witnesses cult predicted a date in 1914, then in 1918, to their great embarrassment.

The Bible does not tell us when He will come. Shortly before His ascension back to heaven, His disciples asked Him when He would come and establish the Kingdom. He told them it was not for them to know the time. However, as He was ascending, angels appeared to them and reaffirmed that he would "come back in the same way [they saw] him go into heaven" (Acts 1:11).

One of my heroes, during and after the time I was in the United States military during World War II, was General Douglas MacArthur. When the Japanese bombed Hawaii on December 7, 1941, General MacArthur was stationed in the Philippines as supreme commander of the United States armed forces in the Pacific.

On February 22, 1942, after the Japanese Army invaded the Philippines, he was ordered by President Franklin Roosevelt to leave the Philippines, and go to Australia. When he left the Philippines he promised, "I shall return!" In 1944 he returned triumphantly. Wading ashore on the beaches of Leyte, he said, "I'm late!"

One day Jesus will return in great glory and universal victory, and **HE** won't be late!

THE PURPOSE OF HIS COMING
The Old Testament gives two lines of prophecy relating to the coming of the Eternal Christ: the suffering servant Redeemer, and the reigning King.

The Suffering Servant Redeemer
The clearest statements concerning His first coming are given to us in the Prophecy of Isaiah:

- He was to be born of a virgin.
- He was to be the Incarnation of God in human flesh.
- His name was to be "Immanuel," meaning "God with us" (Isaiah 7:14).
- This promised One, God incarnate in human flesh, was to be the sacrifice for sin.
- He was prophesied to be the One who would pay our sin-debt and redeem us back to God. He was to pay the penalty for the sins of the world (Isaiah 53) for "the wages of sin is death." And He paid that penalty for every person who will repent and trust Him for salvation.

The passage in Isaiah 53 not only describes the awful suffering through which He was to go; it also describes His attitude and demeanor while experiencing the indescribable suffering.

All of these prophecies mentioned above, and many others, were literally fulfilled at His first coming. But what about the prophecies concerning the reigning King?

Just as surely as the prophecies of His first coming were literally fulfilled, so will the prophecies of His second coming be completely fulfilled. Let's take a look at these prophecies.

The Reigning King

He will come to establish the Kingdom of God on this earth! Many places in the Old Testament record prophesies that when the Messiah comes He will establish a utopian kingdom referred to in Revelation 20:6, as Christ's millennial reign.

The Prophet Daniel writes of the revelation God gave him:

> "...there was given Him (Christ) dominion, and glory, and a kingdom, that all people, nations, and languages, should serve Him: His dominion is an everlasting dominion, which shall not pass away, and His kingdom that which shall not be destroyed"
> —Daniel 7:14

This Scripture assures us that the kingdom of Jesus of Nazareth will be a universal, eternal kingdom over which He will reign as King of kings and Lord of lords (Revelation 17:14; 19:16).

The Apostle Paul exclaims, "God has highly exalted Him and given Him a Name above every name that at the Name of Jesus every knee shall bow..." (Philippians 2:9-10).

What a glorious hope we have. The time will come when, "...the kingdoms of this world have become the kingdom of our Lord and of His Christ, and He shall reign forever and ever" (Revelation 11:15).

The kingdoms of this world are characterized by greed, injustice, hate, war, torture, torment, murder, lust, rape, child abuse, ad infinitum. But this will be absolutely changed when the King of kings comes and establishes the prophesied kingdom of Christ. His will be a kingdom of righteousness, of perfect justice, and universal peace.

When we compare these two kingdoms it is no surprise that the Bible closes with the prayer, "Even so, come Lord Jesus."

Whatever the schedule may be, the thrilling prospect of His personal, visible, victorious return remains our enduring hope.

THEORIES OF HIS SECOND COMING

Theologians have studied and debated end-time events for the last 2000 years, yet there is no consensus regarding the sequence of these events. Three dominant theories have been advocated by godly scholars: Pre-Millennialism, Post-Millennialism, and A-Millennialism. And in recent years there has appeared the theory of Preterism.

The following is a brief summary of each of these:

Pre-Millennialism

After many years of studying the scriptures related to these future events, I believe they will unfold as follows:

1) The Rapture
2) The Judgment Seat of Christ
3) The Great Tribulation
4) The Second Coming of Christ
5) The Millennial Reign of Christ
6) The Second Resurrection
7) The Great White Throne Judgment
8) Eternity

Pre-millennialism teaches that Jesus Christ will come before the millennium in great glory to establish the Kingdom of God on this earth and will reign in perfect righteousness and peace for a thousand years (Revelation 20:4-6).

The following sections discuss each of these important events in more detail:

The Rapture

First Thessalonians 4:13-18 teaches that Christ will come in the air and the dead in Christ shall rise first. That is, those true believers who have died before His return shall be resurrected and given a glorified body (Philippians 3:21; 1 John 3:2; 1 Corinthians 15:51-57). Their glorified bodies will be united with their spirits, which have been with Him since their death.

This is what scripture describes as "the first resurrection" (Revelation 20:5-6). At the same time true believers who are alive at His appearing will be instantly changed into His likeness. They will join those just resurrected and be called up to meet the Lord in the air to be with Him forever and ever.

Can you imagine what it will be like to be "left behind," to suddenly become aware that millions of people have suddenly and mysteriously disappeared? How will the secular media explain it? Imagine a giant aircraft flying through the air. Suddenly, an unbeliever sitting by his wife, who is a believer, looks over and finds her gone. Her clothes are still there; but she is gone. What if the pilots are Christians and all of a sudden the plane is left to crash?

Jesus told us that "...two shall be in the field; one will be taken, and the other left. Two women shall be grinding at the mill; one shall be taken and the other left" (Matthew 24:40-41).

Next are two major events which will occur during this period between the time He comes FOR His Church and the time He comes WITH His church.

The Judgment Seat of Christ (Greek: "Bema")

When Christ comes and takes his Church out of this world, we will stand before the Judgment Seat of Christ to receive our rewards. Second Corinthians 5:10 tells us that every believer shall appear before the "bema" to "... receive the things done in the body, according to what he has done, whether good or bad."

Notice this is not to determine one's destiny. They are already in heaven. It is to determine rewards. In I Corinthians 3:12-13, Paul compares our works while here in this life to a building. These works are to be tested by fire. He uses six elements to describe our works: gold, silver, precious stones, wood, hay, and stubble.

What happens when you test these elements by fire? The first three come out more pure; the last three are burned up. However, notice that Paul says that though the works of some are so valueless that they will be burned up, the people whose works do not stand the test of fire will themselves be saved. The *bema* will be a judgment to give rewards, not to determine one's destiny.

The Great Tribulation

What will happen on earth during this time? In many places in the Bible we are told of a time coming when tribulation, as the world has never known, will cover the entire earth in fulfillment of Daniel's prophecy and the prophecy of Jesus Himself (Daniel 9:24-27; Matthew 24:15-23).

There will emerge a one-world government, currency, and religion, ruled over by one dictator whom the Bible describes as "the man of sin" (2 Thessalonians 2:3), "the beast," the "devil," and "Satan" (Revelation 20:1-2). He is commonly referred to as the Antichrist (see 1 John 2:18,22; 4:3; and 2 John 7). He will have absolute power and those refusing to worship him will be put to death.

According to Daniel's prophecy this will last seven years. At the end of the seven years, as our Lord assembles the multitudes of heaven for His glorious second advent, Satan assembles his armies to confront Him in what will be the battle of the ages.

Our Lord will destroy him and his armies with the sword of His mouth, which is His word, and descend to this earth with His church in great glory and power to establish His millennial kingdom, and we shall reign with Him for a thousand years.

The Millennial Reign of Christ

The Bible has much to say about the conditions on this earth during the millennial (1,000-year) reign of Christ. It will be a reign of peace. Satan and the forces of evil will be cast out at the beginning of the reign.

"He shall judge between the nations, and rebuke many people. They shall beat their swords into plowshares, and their spears into pruning hooks; nation shall not lift up sword against nation, neither shall they learn war anymore" (Isaiah 2:4).

Scripture says even nature itself shall be redeemed and changed (Romans 8:19-22). One of the most graphic descriptions of conditions on the earth during the millennial reign is found in Isaiah 11:6:9:

"The wolf shall dwell with the lamb, the leopard shall lie down with the young goat, the calf and the young lion, and the fatling together; and a little child shall lead them. The cow and the bear shall graze; their young ones shall lie down together; the lion shall eat straw like the ox, the nursing child shall play by the cobra's hole, and the weaned child shall put his hand in the viper's den. They shall not hurt nor destroy in all My holy mountain, for the earth shall be full of the knowledge of the Lord as the waters cover the sea."

No wonder Jesus taught us to pray, "Thy kingdom come!"

The Second Resurrection
At the close of the millennial reign of Christ, the second resurrection will occur, as described in Revelation 21:11-15. This is the resurrection of the spiritually lost, those who have died in their sin.

The Great White Throne Judgment
Here, all those lost souls who were raised in the second resurrection will each and everyone stand before God at what the Bible calls "The Great White Throne Judgment" in Revelation 20:11-15. There they will receive their reward, which is eternal punishment and separation from God in a place Jesus called hell (Luke 16:19-31).

Eternity
Eternity begins with all the saved from all ages with our Lord and Savior in heaven, and the lost in the place called hell with the devil and his angels. It is with sadness in my heart that I draw attention to this last matter.

In the words of our Lord, (Ezekiel 18:31-32) "Why should you die…for I have no pleasure in the death of one who dies. Therefore, turn and live."

I have given more than 65 years of my life trying to persuade people to turn from their sins to the only Savior God has given to the world, the Lord Jesus Christ.

Post-Millennialism

This is the theory that the millennium—the utopian period of peace and righteousness—will be brought about by the church through world evangelism and education. Christ will return after the millennium.

This was the dominant eschatology toward the end of the 19th century and the early years of the 20th century. It was a time of idealism seldom seen in history. World missions were reaching out to the ends of the earth. Great Christian theologians fervently believed that world evangelism and Christian education would bring this about.

For example, the leading, most popular Christian magazine of that time was "The Christian Century." Dr. B. H. Carroll, the founder and first president of the Southwestern Baptist Theological Seminary was a post-millennialist.

However it is reported that shortly before his death he told his successor, Dr. L. R. Scarborough, "It looks like you Pre-millennialists are right after all."

At the same time the optimists were proclaiming their vision of a utopian society coming as a result of man's efforts, C.H. Spurgeon proclaimed that the world was more likely to sink into a pandemonium than rise into a millennium.

What caused this change of mind? Catastrophic events crushed their optimist outlook: 1917 saw World War I; 1929 experienced the crash of the stock market and ushered in what historians call "the great depression;" 1938 marked the beginning of World War II, when Hitler's military might launched a blood bath across Europe that soon spread over most of the earth.

There are not many post-millennialists left in the theological world. When one evaluates world conditions during the last one hundred years we can see why. The twentieth century was the bloodiest century in history.

A-Millennialism

This theory teaches that the concept of a millennium in the Bible is symbolic. There will be no millennium. This is a very popular theory in most seminaries today. Proponents of this theory saw the disappointment of post-millennialism and the extremes of some advocates of "millennial-dawnism," such as the cult Jehovah's Witnesses, and developed a theology of symbolism.

It presents the concept that at a certain time in the future Jesus will return; there will be one general resurrection and one general judgment. The world as we know it will come to an end, and eternity will begin. This is a very simple theory; however, it ignores masses of scripture concerning the prophecies of universal peace on this earth, and the reign of Jesus Christ on this earth as He establishes a universal kingdom of righteousness.

Preterism (Latin = "Last")

This theory teaches that the prophecies of the book of Revelation were fulfilled in 70 AD, in the destruction of Jerusalem. Moderate preterists claim they still believe in the

Second Coming of Christ, but still insist on interpreting the Olivet Discourse (Matthew 24), and the book of Revelation as already fulfilled. Many teachers of this theory believe:

1) Nero was the Anti-Christ. There will be no future individual Anti-Christ.
2) The great tribulation occurred when the Roman army besieged and destroyed Jerusalem in AD 66-70.
3) Christ returned in the clouds in AD 70 to witness the destruction of Jerusalem.
4) Armageddon happened in AD 70.
5) Satan is already bound in the abyss and cannot hinder the spread of the gospel.
6) Some preterists equate the Church Age as the millennium.

As with other theories, this teaching ignores and symbolizes masses of Scripture.

SUMMARY STATEMENT

This summarizes what I understand to be the various dominant theories of the last-times events and Second Advent of our Lord Jesus Christ to this earth. It is obvious as you have read this that I believe the pre-millennial position is best supported by the Word of God.

Whatever the schedule may be, the thrilling prospect of His personal, visible, victorious return remains our enduring hope.

9

MY TESTIMONY

I have not written to challenge the mind of the professional theologian or philosopher. I have written for the mind and heart of the average layperson. I have summarized these truths, as I understand them, in language anyone can understand.

Christians enjoy something no other people on earth possess; an abiding and eternal hope based upon, not the philosophies of man, but upon the eternal truth revealed to us by the eternal, living God of the universe.

We are the redeemed family of God, made so by the death and resurrection of our Lord Jesus Christ. He promised us that, one day, we will be conformed to the very image of the resurrected Christ and live with Him throughout eternity.

- I believe that the Bible is the inspired, inerrant, word of God and is our only authentic revelation of the Person, work, will, and purposes of God. I believe that God chose certain men and moved them along by the Holy Spirit to write exactly what He wanted us to know and believe.

- I believe there is One eternal, omnipotent, omniscient, and omnipresent God Who is Spirit. I believe that He has revealed Himself as Father, Son, and Holy Spirit; one God revealed in triunity.
- Jesus of Nazareth was the Eternal God of the universe incarnate in a man. He was born of the Virgin Mary, conceived by the Holy Spirit. He lived a perfect life, willingly took upon Himself the sins of mankind and died a substitutionary death on the cross to pay in full the penalty for sin for any and every one who will repent of their sin and place their faith in Him. I believe that He arose bodily from the dead, and after revealing Himself to hundreds of people, ascended back to heaven where He sits as our High Priest awaiting the day when He will come the second time in great glory to establish the Kingdom of God on this earth and reign for a thousand years in perfect peace and righteousness.
- I believe the Holy Spirit, the third Person of the Triunity, is in our world this very moment, in great power, equipping the church to fulfill our Lord's will and purpose.
- I believe that sinful mankind is saved by God's grace through faith plus nothing. I believe that any person, regardless of who he or she is or what he or she has done, who will repent of sin and place faith in the crucified, risen Savior, Jesus Christ will be forgiven and spend eternity in heaven with the triune God.

I am grateful for the privilege I have had to teach and preach these truths to thousands of people on six continents of this world. Thousands of them have believed these truths, and placed their faith in our Lord Jesus Christ. What joy it will be to reunite and spend eternity with them!

To God be the glory, great things He has done! Greater still will be what He will do when our Lord Jesus returns in all

His glory to usher in the eternal Kingdom of God in visible perfection.

A PERSONAL APPEAL

It is my prayer that this small book will be used of our Lord to do at least two things:

1) First, that it will edify and strengthen young, growing Christians in their faith;
2) And second, that many unbelievers who are searching for truth will come to know Jesus Christ as Savior and Lord.

Please share your copy with someone you know who could benefit from these truths.